Under Cove

Wyndham Martyn, Roi Cooper Megrue

Alpha Editions

This edition published in 2024

ISBN : 9789362092229

Design and Setting By
Alpha Editions
www.alphaedis.com
Email - info@alphaedis.com

As per information held with us this book is in Public Domain.
This book is a reproduction of an important historical work. Alpha Editions uses the best technology to reproduce historical work in the same manner it was first published to preserve its original nature. Any marks or number seen are left intentionally to preserve its true form.

Contents

CHAPTER ONE ....- 1 -
CHAPTER TWO ....- 13 -
CHAPTER THREE ....- 23 -
CHAPTER FOUR ....- 29 -
CHAPTER FIVE ....- 37 -
CHAPTER SEVEN ....- 60 -
CHAPTER EIGHT ....- 68 -
CHAPTER NINE ....- 87 -
CHAPTER TEN ....- 97 -
CHAPTER ELEVEN ....- 105 -
CHAPTER TWELVE ....- 116 -
CHAPTER THIRTEEN ....- 126 -
CHAPTER FOURTEEN ....- 138 -
CHAPTER FIFTEEN ....- 144 -
CHAPTER SIXTEEN ....- 151 -
CHAPTER SEVENTEEN ....- 158 -

CHAPTER ONE

PARIS wears her greenest livery and puts on her most gracious airs in early summer. When the National Fete commemorative of the Bastille's fall has gone, there are few Parisians of wealth or leisure who remain in their city. Trouville, Deauville, Etretat and other pleasure cities claim them and even the bourgeoisie hie them to their summer villas.

The city is given up to those tourists from America and England whom Paris still persists in calling *Les Cooks* in memory of that enterprising blazer of cheap trails for the masses. Your true Parisian and the stranger who has stayed within the city's gates to know her well, find themselves wholly out of sympathy with the eager crowds who follow beaten tracks and absorb topographical knowledge from guide-books.

Monty Vaughan was an American who knew his Paris in all months but those two which are sacred to foreign travelers, and it irritated him one blazing afternoon in late July to be persistently mistaken for a tourist and offered silly useless toys and plans of the Louvre. The *camelots*, those shrewd itinerant merchants of the Boulevards, pestered him continually. These excellent judges of human nature saw in him one who lacked the necessary harshness to drive them away and made capital of his good nature.

He was a slim, pleasant-looking man of five and twenty, to whom the good things of this world had been vouchsafed, with no effort on his part to obtain them; and in spite of this he preserved a certain frank and boyish charm which had made him popular all his life.

Presently on his somewhat aimless wanderings he came down the Avenue de l'Opéra and took a seat under the awning and ordered an innocuous drink. He was in a city where he had innumerable friends, but they had all left for the seashore and this loneliness was unpleasant to his friendly spirit. But even in the Café de Paris he was not to be left alone and he was regarded as fair game by alert hawkers. One would steal up to his table and deposit a little measure of olives and plead for two sous in exchange. Another would place some nuts by his side and demand a like amount. And when they had been driven forth and he had lighted a cigarette, he observed watching him with professional eagerness a *ramasseur de megot*, one of those men who make a livelihood of picking up the butts of cigars and cigarettes and selling them.

When Monty flung down the half-smoked cigarette in hope that the man would go away he was annoyed to find that the fellow was congratulating himself that here was a tourist worth following, who smoked not the wispy attenuated cigarettes of the native but one worth harvesting. He probed for it with his long stick under the table and stood waiting for another.

The heat, the absence of his friends and the knowledge that he must presently dine alone had brought the usually placid Monty into a wholly foreign frame of mind and he rose abruptly and stalked down the Avenue.

A depressed-looking sandwich-man, bearing a device which read, "One can laugh uproariously at the Champs Elysées every night during the summer months," blocked his way, and permitted a woman selling fans of the kind known to the *camelots* as *les petits vents du nord* to thrust one upon him. "Monsieur does not comprehend our heat in Paris," she said. "Buy a little north wind. Two sous for a little north wind."

Monty thrust a franc in her hand and turned quickly from her to carom against a tall well-dressed man who was passing. As Monty began to utter his apology the look of gloom dropped from his face and he seized the stranger's hand and shook it heartily.

"Steve, old man!" he cried, "what luck to find you amid this mob! I've been feeling like a poor shipwrecked orphan, and here you come to my rescue again."

The man he addressed as Steve seemed just as pleased to behold Monty Vaughan. The two were old comrades from the days at their preparatory school and had met little during the past five years. Monty's ecstatic welcome was a pleasant reminder of happy days that were gone.

"I might ask what you are doing here," Steven Denby returned. "I imagined you to be sunning yourself in Newport or Bar Harbor, not doing Paris in July."

"I've been living here for two years," Monty explained, when they were sheltered from interruption at the café Monty had just left.

"Doing what?"

Monty looked at him with a diffident smile. "I suppose you'll grin just like everybody else. I'm here to learn foreign banking systems. My father says it will do me good."

Denby laughed. "I'll bet you know less about it than I do." The idea of Monty Vaughan, heir to the Vaughan millions, working like a clerk in the Crédit Lyonnais was amusing.

"Does your father make you work all summer?" he demanded.

"I'm not working now," Monty explained. "I never do unless I feel like it. I'm waiting for a friend who is sailing with me on the Mauretania next week and I've just had a wire to say she'll be here to-morrow."

"She!" echoed Denby. "Have you married without my knowledge or consent? Or is this a honey-moon trip you are taking?"

A look of sadness came into the younger man's face.

"I shall never marry," he returned.

But Steven Denby knew him too well to take such expressions of gloom as final. "Nonsense," he cried. "You are just the sort they like. You're inclined to believe in people too much if you like them, and a husband who believes in his wife as you will in yours is a treasure. They'll fight for you, Monty, when you get home again. For all you know the trap is already baited."

"Trap!" Monty cried reproachfully. "I've been trying to make a girl catch me for three years now and she won't."

"Do you mean you've been finally turned down?" Steven Denby asked curiously. It was difficult to suppose that a man of his friend's wealth and standing would experience much trouble in offering heart and fortune.

"I haven't asked yet," Monty admitted. "I've been on the verge of it hundreds of times, but she always laughs as I'm coming around to it, and someone comes in or something happens and I've never done it." He sighed with the deprecating manner of the devout lover. "If you'd only seen her, Steve, you'd see what mighty little chance I stood. I feel it's a bit of impertinence to ask a girl like that to marry me."

Steven patted him on the arm. "You're just the same," he said, "exactly the silly old Monty I used to know. Next time you see your charmer, risk being impertinent and ask her to marry you. Women hate modesty nowadays. It's just a confession of failure and we're all hitched up to success. I don't know the girl you are speaking of but when you get home again instead of declaring your great unworthiness, tell her you've left Paris and its pleasures simply to marry her. Say that the Bourse begged you to remain and guide the nation through a financial panic, but you left them weeping and flew back on a fast Cunarder."

"I believe you are right," Monty said. "I'll do it. I ought to have done it years ago. Alice is frightfully disappointed with me."

"Who is Alice?" the other demanded. "The lady you're crossing with on the Mauretania?"

"Yes," said Monty. "A good pal of mine; one of those up-to-date women of the world who know what to do and say at the right moment. She's a sort of elder sister to me. You'll like her, Steve."

Denby doubted it but pursued the subject no further. He conceived Alice to be one of those capable managing women who do so much good in the world and give so little pleasure.

"What are you doing in Paris now?" Monty presently demanded. It occurred to him that it was odd that Denby, too, should be in the city now.

"Writing a book on the Race Courses of the World," he said, smiling. "I am now in the midst of Longchamps."

Monty looked at him doubtfully. He had never known that his friend had any literary aspirations, but he did remember him as one who, if he did not choose to tell, would invent airy fairy fancies to deceive.

"I don't believe it," he said.

"You are quite right," Denby admitted. "You've got the key to the mystery. I'll confess that I have been engaged to guard Mona Lisa. Suspicious looking tourists such as you engage my special attention. Don't get offended, Monty," he added, "I'm just wandering through the city on my way to England and that's the truth, simple as it may seem. I was desolate and your pleasing countenance as you bought a franc's worth of north wind was good to see. I wondered if you'd remember me."

"Remember you!" Monty snorted. "Am I the kind to forget a man who saved my life?"

"Who did that?" Denby inquired.

"Why, you did," he returned, "You pulled me out of the Nashua river at school!"

The other man laughed. "Why, it wasn't five feet deep there."

"I can drown anywhere," Monty returned firmly. "You saved my life and I've never had the opportunity to do anything in return."

"The time will come," Denby said lightly. "You'll get a mysterious message sometime and it will be up to you to rescue me from dreadful danger."

"I'd like to," the other retorted, "but I'm not sure I'm cut out for that rescue business."

"Have you ever been—" Denby hesitated. "Have you ever been in any sort of danger?"

"Yes," Monty replied promptly, "but you pulled me out."

"Please don't go about repeating it," Denby entreated, "I have enemies enough without being blamed for pulling you out of the Nashua river."

Monty looked at him in astonishment. Here was the most popular boy in Groton School complaining of enemies. Monty felt a thrill that had something of enjoyment in it. His own upbringing had been so free from any danger and his parents had safeguarded him from so much trouble that he had found life insipid at times. Yet here was a man talking of enemies. It was fascinating.

"Do you mean it?" he demanded.

"Why not?" said Denby, rolling himself a cigarette.

"You hadn't any at school," Monty insisted.

"That was a dozen years ago nearly," Denby insisted. "Since then—" He paused. "My career wouldn't interest you, my financial expert, but I am safe in saying I have accumulated a number of persons who do not wish me well."

"You must certainly meet Alice," Monty asserted. "She's like you. She often says I'm the only really uninteresting person she's fond of."

Denby assured himself that Alice would not interest him in the slightest degree and made haste to change the subject, but Monty held on to his chosen course.

"We'll all dine together to-morrow night," he cried.

"I'm afraid I'm too busy."

"Too busy to dine with Alice Harrington when you've the opportunity?" Monty exclaimed. "Are you a woman-hater?"

A more observant man might have noted the sudden change in expression that the name Harrington produced in Steven Denby. He had previously been bored at the idea of meeting a woman who he concluded would be eager to impart her guide-book knowledge. Alice evidently had meant nothing to him, but Alice Harrington roused a sudden interest.

"Not by any chance Mrs. Michael Harrington?" he queried.

Monty nodded. "The same. She and Michael are two of the best friends I have. He's a great old sport and she's hurrying back because he has to stay on and can't get over this year." Monty flushed becomingly. "I'm going back with her because Nora is going to stay down in Long Island with them."

"Introduce me to Nora," Denby insisted. "She is a new motif in your jocund song. Who is Nora, what is she, that Monty doth commend her?"

"She's the girl," Monty explained. He sighed. "If you only knew how pretty she was, you wouldn't talk about a trap being baited. I don't think women are the good judges they pretend to be!"

"Why not?" Denby demanded.

"Because Alice says she'd accept me and I don't believe I stand a ghost of a chance."

"Women are the only judges," Denby assured him seriously. "If I were you I'd bank on your friend Alice every time."

"Then you'll dine with me to-morrow?" Monty asked.

"Of course. You don't suppose I am going to lose sight of you, do you?"

And Monty, grateful that this admired old school friend was so ready to join him, forgot the previous excuse about inability to spare the time.

"That's fine," he exclaimed. "But what are we going to do to-night?"

"You are going to dine with me," Denby told him. "I haven't seen you, let me see," he reflected, "I haven't seen you for about ten years and I want to talk over the old days. What do you say to trying some of Marguery's *sole à la Normandie?*"

During the course of the dinner Monty talked frankly and freely about his past, present and future. Denby learned that in view of the great wealth which would devolve upon him, his father had determined that he should become grounded in finance. When he had finished, he reflected that while he had opened his soul to his old friend, his old friend had offered no explanation of what in truth brought him to Europe, or why he had for almost a decade dropped out of his old set.

"But what have you been doing?" Monty gathered courage to ask. "I've told you all about me and mine, Steve."

"There isn't much to tell," Denby responded slowly. "I left Groton because my father died. I'm afraid he wasn't a shrewd man like your father, Monty. He was one of the last relics of New York's brown-stone age and he tried to keep the pace when the marble age came in. He couldn't do it."

"You were going into the diplomatic service," Monty reminded him. "You used to specialize in modern languages, I remember. I suppose you had to give that up."

"I had to try to earn my own living," Denby explained, "and diplomacy doesn't pay much at first even if you have the luck to get an appointment."

Monty looked at him shrewdly. He saw a tall, well set up man who had every appearance of affluence.

"You've done pretty well for yourself."

Denby smiled, "The age demands that a man put up a good appearance. A financier like you ought not to be deceived."

Monty leaned over the table. "Steve, old man," he said, a trifle nervously, "I don't want to butt in on your private affairs, but if you ever want any money you'll offend me if you don't let me know. I've too much and that's a fact. Except for putting a bit on Michael's horses when they run and a bit of a flutter occasionally at Monte Carlo I don't get rid of much of it. I've got heaps. Do you want any?"

"Monty," the other man said quietly, "you haven't altered. You are still the same generous boy I remember and it's good for a man like me to know that. I don't need any money, but if ever I do I'll come to you."

Monty sighed with relief. His old idol was not hard up and he had not been offended at the suggestion. It was a good world and he was happy.

"Steve," he asked presently, "what did you mean about having enemies and being in danger? That was a joke, wasn't it?"

"We most of us have enemies," Steven said lightly, "and we are all in danger. For all you know ptomaines are gathering their forces inside you even now."

"You didn't mean that," Monty said positively. "You were serious. What enemies?"

"Enemies I have made in the course of my work," the other returned.

"Well, what work is it?" Monty queried. It was odd, he thought, that Denby would not let him into so harmless a secret as the nature of his work. He felt an unusual spirit of persistence rising within him. "What work?" he repeated.

Denby shrugged his shoulders. "You might call it a little irregular," he said in a lowered voice. "You represent high finance. Your father is one of the big men in American affairs. You probably have his set views on things. I don't want to shock you, Monty."

"Shock be damned!" cried Monty in an aggrieved voice. "I'm tired of having to accommodate myself to other people's views."

Denby looked at him with mock wonder.

"Monty in revolt at the established order of things is a most remarkable phenomenon. Have you a pirate in your family tree that you sigh for sudden change and a life on the ocean wave?"

Monty laughed. "I don't want to do anything like that but I'm tired of a life that is always the same. You've enemies. I don't believe I've one. I'd like to have an enemy, Steve. I'd like to feel I was in danger; it would be a change after being wrapped in wool all my life. You've probably seen the world in a way I never shall. I've been on a personally conducted tour, which isn't the same thing."

"Not by a long shot," Steven Denby agreed. "But," he added, "why should you want to take the sort of risks that I have had to take, when there's no need? I have been in danger pretty often, Monty, and I shall again. Why? Because I have my living to make and that way suits me best. You notice I am sitting with my back to the wall so that none can come behind me. I do that because two revengeful gentlemen have sworn bloodthirsty oaths to relieve my soul of its body."

Monty tingled with a certain pleasurable apprehension which had never before visited him. He was experiencing in real life what had only revealed itself before in novels or on the stage.

"What are they like?" he demanded in a low voice, looking around.

"Disappointing, I'm afraid," Steven answered. "You are looking for a tall man with a livid scar running from temple to chin and a look before which even a waiter would blanch. Both my men have mild expressions and wouldn't attract a second glance, but they'll either get me or I'll get them."

"Steve!" Monty cried. "What did they do?"

Denby made a careless gesture. "It was over a money matter," he explained.

Monty thought for a moment in silence. Never had his conventional lot seemed less attractive to him. He approached the subject again as do timid men who fearfully hang on the outskirts of a street fight, unwilling to miss what they have not the heart to enjoy.

"I wish some excitement like that would come my way," he sighed.

"Excitement? Go to Monte and break the bank. Become the Jaggers of your country."

"There's no danger in that," Monty answered almost peevishly.

"Nor of it," laughed his friend.

"That's just the way it always is," Monty complained. "Other fellows have all the fun and I just hear about it."

Denby looked at him shrewdly and then leaned across the table.

"So you want some fun?" he queried.

"I do," the other said firmly.

"Do you think you've got the nerve?" Steven demanded.

Monty hesitated. "I don't want to be killed," he admitted. "What is it?"

"I didn't tell you how I made a living, but I hinted my ways were a bit irregular. What I have to propose is also a trifle out of the usual. The law and the equator are both imaginary lines, Monty, and I'm afraid my little expedition may get off the line. I suppose you don't want to hear any more, do you?"

Monty's eyes were shining with excitement. "I'm going to hear everything you've got to say," he asserted.

"It means I've got to put myself in your power in a way," Denby said hesitatingly, "but I'll take a chance because you're the kind of man who can keep things secret."

"I am," Monty said fervently. "Just you try me out, Steve!"

"It has to do with a string of pearls," Denby explained, "and I'm afraid I shall disappoint you when I tell you I'm proposing to pay for them just as any one else might do."

"Oh!" said Monty. "Is that all?"

"When I buy these pearls, as you will see me do, with Bank of France notes, they belong to me, don't they?"

"Sure they do," Monty exclaimed. "They are yours to do as you like with."

"That's exactly how I feel about it," Denby said. "It happens to be my particular wish to take those pearls back to my native land."

"Then for heaven's sake do it," Monty advised. "What's hindering you?"

"A number of officious prying hirelings called customs officials. They admit that the pearls aren't improved by the voyage, yet they want me to pay a duty of twenty per cent. if I take them home with me."

"So you're going to smuggle 'em," Monty cried. "That's a cinch!"

"Is it?" Denby returned slowly. "It might have been in the past, but things aren't what they were in the good old days. They're sending even society women to jail now as well as fining them. The whole service from being a joke has become efficient. I tell you there's risk in it, and believe me, Monty, I know."

"Where would I come in?" the other asked.

"You'd come in on the profits," Denby explained, "and you'd be a help as well."

"Profits?" Monty queried. "What profits?"

Denby laughed. "You simple child of finance, do you think I'm buying a million-franc necklace to wear about my own fair neck? I can sell it at a fifty thousand dollar profit in the easiest sort of way. There are avenues by which I can get in touch with the right sort of buyers without any risk. My only difficulty is getting the thing through the customs. It's up to you to get your little excitement if you're game."

Monty shut his eyes and felt as one does who is about to plunge for the first swim of the season into icy water. It was one thing to talk about danger in the abstract and another to have it suddenly offered him.

Steven had talked calmly about men who wanted to part his soul from his body as though such things were in no way out of the ordinary. Suppose these desperate beings assumed Montague Vaughan to be leagued with Steven Denby and as such worthy of summary execution! But he put aside these fears and turned to his old friend.

"I'm game," he said, "but I'm not in this for the profits." Now he was once committed to it, his spirits began to rise. "What about the danger?" he asked.

"There may be none at all," the other admitted. "If there is it may be slight. If by any chance it is known to certain crooks that I have it with me there may be an attempt to get it. Naturally they won't ask me pleasantly to hand it over, they'll take it by force. That's one danger. Then I may be trailed by the customs people, who could be warned through secret channels that I have it and am purposing to smuggle it in."

"But what can I do?" Monty asked. He was anxious to help but saw little opportunity.

"You can tell me if any people follow me persistently while we're together in Paris or whether the same man happens to sit next to me at cafés or any shows we take in." He paused a moment, "By Jove, Monty, this means I shall have to book a passage on the Mauretania!"

"That's the best part of it," Monty cried.

"But Mrs. Harrington," Denby said. "She might not like it."

"Alice can't choose a passenger list," Monty exclaimed; "and she'll be glad to have any old friend of mine."

"That's a thing I want to warn you of," the other man said. "I don't want you to give away too many particulars about me. Don't persist in that fable about my saving your life. Know me just enough to vouch to her that I'm housebroken but don't get to the point where we have to discuss common friends. I have my reasons, Monty, which I'll explain later on. I don't court publicity this trip and I don't want any reporter to jump aboard at Quarantine and get interested in me."

"I see," cried the sapient Monty and felt he was plunging at last into dark doings and mysterious depths. "But how am I to warn you if you're followed? I shall be with you and we ought not to let on that we know." He felt in that moment the hours he had spent with detective novels had been time well spent.

"We must devise something," Denby agreed, "and something simple." He meditated for a moment. "Here's an idea. If you should think I'm being followed or you want me to understand that something unusual is up, just say without any excitement, 'Will you have a cigarette, Dick?'"

"But why 'Dick,'" Monty cried, "when you're Steve!"

"For that very reason," Denby explained. "If you said Steve merely I shouldn't notice it, but if you say Dick I shall be on the *qui vive* at once."

"Great idea!" cried his fellow conspirator enthusiastically. "When do you buy them?"

"I've an appointment at Cartier's at eleven. Want to come?"

"You bet I do," Monty asserted, "I'm going through with it from start to finish."

He looked at his friend a little anxiously. "What is the worst sort of a finish we might expect if the luck ran against us?"

"As you won't come in on the profits, you shan't take any risks," Denby said. "If you agree to help me as we suggested that's all I require of you. In case I should not get by, you can explain me away as a passing acquaintance merely. Don't kick against the umpire's decision," he commanded. "If they halved the sentence because two were in it I might claim your help all the way, but they'd probably double it for conspiracy, so you'd be a handicap. You'll get a run for your money, Monty, all right."

"I'm not so sure," said Monty doubtfully.

Denby fell into the bantering style the other knew so well. "There's one thing I'll warn you about," he said. "If a very beautiful young woman makes your acquaintance on board, by accident of course, don't tell her what life seems to you as is your custom. She may be an agent of the Russian secret police with an assignment to take you to Siberia. She may force you to marry her at a pistol's point and cost your worthy progenitor a million. Be careful, Monty. You're in a wicked world and you've a sinful lot of money, and these big ships attract all that is brightest and best in the criminal's Who's Who."

Monty shivered a bit. "I never thought of that," he said innocently.

"Then you'd better begin now," his mentor suggested, "and have for once a voyage where you won't be bored."

He glanced at the clock. "It's later than I thought and I have to be up early. I'll walk to your hotel."

During the short walk Monty glanced apprehensively over his shoulder a score of times. Out of the shadows it seemed to him that mysterious men stared evilly and banded themselves together until a procession followed the two Americans. But Denby paid no sort of attention to these problematic followers.

"Wait till I've got the pearls on me," he whispered mischievously. "Then you'll see some fun."

CHAPTER TWO

ALTHOUGH the carriages and automobiles of the wealthy were no longer three deep in the Rue de la Paix, as they had been earlier in the season, this ravishing thoroughfare was crowded with foot-passengers as Monty and his friend made their way under the red and white awnings of the shops into Cartier's.

The transaction took very little time. The manager of the place seemed to be expecting his client, to whom he accorded the respect that even a Rue de la Paix jeweler may pay to a million-franc customer. Bank of France notes of high denominations were passed to him and Steven Denby received a small, flat package and walked out into the sunshine with it.

"Now," said the owner of the pearls, "guard me as you would your honor, Monty; the sport begins, and I am now probably pursued by a half dozen of the super-crooks of high class fiction."

"I wish you'd be serious," Monty said plaintively.

"I am," Denby assured him. "But I rely on your protection, so feel more light-hearted than I should otherwise."

"You are laughing at me," Monty protested.

"I want you to look a little less like a detected criminal," Denby returned. "If I happened to be a detective after a criminal I should arrest you on sight. You keep looking furtively about as though you'd done murder and bloodhounds were on your track."

"Well, they are on our track," Monty said excitedly, and then whispered thrillingly: "Have a cigarette, Dick." There was trembling triumph in his voice. He felt he had justified himself in his friend's eyes.

"What is it?" Denby asked with no show of excitement.

"There was a man in Cartier's who watched us all the time," Monty confided. "He is on our trail now. We're being shadowed, Steve. It's all up!"

"Nonsense!" his companion cried. "There's nothing compromising in buying a pearl necklace. I didn't steal it."

Suddenly he turned around and looked at the man Monty indicated. His face cleared. "That's Harlow. He's one of Cartier's clerks, who looks after American women's wants. Don't worry about him."

By this time the two had come to the Tuileries, that paradise for the better class Parisian children. Denby pointed to a seat. "Sit down there," he commanded, "while I see what Harlow wants."

Obediently Monty took a seat and watched the man he had mistaken for a detective from the corner of his eye. Denby chatted confidentially with him for fully five minutes and then, it seemed to the watcher, passed a small packet into his hand. The man nodded a friendly adieu and walked rapidly out of sight. For a few seconds Denby stood watching and then rejoined his friend.

"Anything the matter?" the timorous one demanded eagerly.

"Why should there be?" Denby returned. "Don't worry, Monty, there's nothing to get nervous about yet."

Monty remembered the confidential conversation between the two.

"He seemed to have a lot to tell you," he insisted.

Denby smiled. "He did; but he came as a friend. Harlow wanted to warn me that while I was buying the necklace a stranger was mightily interested and asked Harlow what he knew about me."

"There you are," Monty gasped excitedly, "I told you it was all up. Did Harlow know who the man was?"

"He suspected him of being a customs spy. Our customs service takes the civilized world as its hunting ground and Paris is specially beloved of it."

"What are you going to do?" Monty asked when he had looked suspiciously at an amiable old priest who went ambling by. "They'll get you."

"They may," Denby said, "but the interested gentleman at Cartier's won't."

"But he knows all about you," Monty persisted. "It will be dead easy."

"He doesn't," the other returned. "Harlow took the liberty of transforming me into an Argentine ranch owner of unbounded wealth about to purchase a mansion in the Parc Monceau."

"That was mighty good of him," Monty cried in relief. "That fellow Harlow is certainly all right."

Denby smiled a trifle oddly, Monty thought. "His kind ways have won him a thousand dollars," he returned. "Did you see me pass him something?"

Monty nodded.

"Well, that was five thousand francs. I passed it to him, not in the least because I believe in the mythical stranger—"

"What do you mean?" the amazed Monty exclaimed. It seemed to him he was getting lost in a world of whose existence he had been unaware.

"Simply this," Denby told him, "that I disbelieve Harlow's story and am not as easily impressed by kind faces as you are. I think Harlow's inquisitive stranger was a fake."

Monty looked at him with a superior air. "And you mean to say," he said with the air of one who has studied financial systems, "that you handed over a thousand dollars without verifying it? I call that being easy."

"It's this way," Denby explained patiently. "Harlow knows I have the necklace and he's in a position to know on what boat I sail. If I had not remembered that I owed him five thousand francs just now he might have informed the customs that I had bought a million-franc necklace and I should have been marked down as one to whom a special search must be made if I didn't declare it."

"But if he's a clerk in Cartier's what has he to do with the customs?" Monty asked.

"Perhaps he is underpaid," the other returned. "Perhaps he is extravagant—I've seen him at the races and noticed that he patronized the *pari mutuel*—perhaps he has a wife and twelve children. I'll leave it to you to decide, but I dare not take a risk."

Monty shivered. "It looks to me as if we were going to have a hell of a time."

"A little excitement possibly," Denby said airily, "but nothing to justify language like that, though. You ought to have been with me last year at Buenos Ayres, Monty, and I could have shown you some sport."

"I don't think I'm built for a life like that," Monty admitted, and then reflected that this friend of his was an exceedingly mysterious being of whose adult life and adventures he knew nothing. For an uneasy moment he hoped his father would never discover this association, but there soon prevailed the old boyish spirit of hero-worship. Steven Denby might not conform to some people's standards, but he felt certain he would do nothing criminal. One had to live, Monty reflected, and his father complained constantly of hard times.

"What sort of sport was it?" he hazarded.

"It had to do with the secret of a torpedo controlled by wireless," Denby said. "A number of governments were after it and there collected in Buenos Ayres the choicest collection of high-grade adventurers that I have ever seen. Some day when I'm through with this pearl trouble I'll tell you about it."

But what Denby had carelessly termed "pearl trouble" was quite sufficient for the less experienced man. He had a vivid imagination, more vivid now than at any period of his career. Paris was full of Apaches, he knew, and not all spent their days lying in the sun outside the barriers. Supposing one sprang from behind a tree and fell upon Denby and seized the precious package whose outline was discernible through the breast pocket of his coat. Monty suddenly took upon himself the rôle of an adviser.

"It's no use taking unnecessary risks," he said. "I saw you put those pearls in your breast pocket, and there were at least six people who had the same opportunity as I. It's just putting temptation in the way of a thief."

"I welcome this outbreak of caution on your part," said Denby, laughing at his expression of anxiety, "but you'll need it on board ship most. The greatest danger is that a couple of crooks may rob me and then pitch me overboard. Monty, for the sake of our boyhood recollections, don't let them throw me overboard."

"Now you are laughing at me," Monty said a trifle sulkily.

"What do you want me to do?" Denby demanded.

"Put those pearls in some other place," he returned stubbornly.

Denby made a pass or two in the air as conjurers do when they perform their marvels.

"It's done," he cried. "From what part of my anatomy or yours shall I produce them?"

"There you go," Monty exclaimed helplessly, "you won't be serious. I'm getting all on the jump."

"A cigarette will soothe you," Denby told him, taking a flat leathern pouch from his pocket and offering it to the other.

"I can't roll 'em," Monty protested.

"Then a look at my tobacco has a soothing effect," the elder man insisted. "I grow it in my private vineyard in Ruritania."

Monty turned back the leather flap to look at his friend's private brand and saw nestling in a place where once tobacco might have reposed a necklace of pearls for which a million of francs had been paid.

"Good Lord!" Monty gasped. "How did you do it?"

"A correspondence school course in legerdemain," Steven explained. "It comes in handy at times."

"But I didn't see you do it and I was watching."

"An unconscious tribute to my art," Denby replied. "Monty, I thank you."

Monty grew less anxious. If Steven had all sorts of tricks up his sleeve there was no reason to suppose he must fail.

"I don't think you need my advice," he admitted. "It doesn't seem I can help you."

"You may be able to help a great deal," Denby said more seriously, "but I don't want you to act as if you were a criminal. Pass it off easily. Of course,"—he hesitated,—"I've had more experience in this sort of thing than you, and am more used to being up against it, but it will never do if you look as anxiously at everybody on the Mauretania as you do at the passers-by here. You can help me particularly by observing if I am the subject of special scrutiny."

"That will be a cinch," Monty asserted.

"Then start right away," his mentor commanded. "We have been under observation for the last five minutes by someone I've never laid eyes on before."

"Good Lord!" Monty cried. "It was that old priest who stared at us. I knew he was a fake. That was a wig he had on!"

"Try again," Denby suggested. "It happens to be a woman and a very handsome one. As we went into Cartier's she passed in a taxi. I only thought then that she was a particularly charming American or English woman out on a shopping expedition. When we came out she was in one of those expensive *couturier's* opposite, standing at an upper window which commands a view of Cartier's door. They may have been coincidences, but at the present moment, although we are sauntering along the Champs Elysées, she is pursuing us in another taxi. She has passed us once. When she went by she told the chauffeur to turn, but he was going at such a pace that he couldn't pull up in time. He has just turned and is now bearing down on us. Take a look at the lady, Monty, so you will know her again."

A sense of dreadful responsibility settled on Montague Vaughan. He was now entering upon his rôle of Denby's aid and must in a few seconds be brought face to face with what was unquestionably an adventuress of the highest class. He knew all about them from fiction. She would have the faintest foreign accent, be wholly charming and free from vulgarity, and yet like Keats' creation be a *belle dame sans merci*. But, he wondered uneasily, what would be his rôle if his friend fell victim to her charms?

He was startled out of his vain imaginings when Denby exclaimed: "By all that's wonderful, she seems to know one of us, and it's not I! You're the fortunate man, Monty."

A pretty woman with good features and laughing eyes was certainly looking out of a taxi and smiling right at him. And when he realized this, Monty's depression was lifted and he sprang forward to meet her. "It's Alice," he cried.

Denby, following more leisurely, was introduced to her.

"I came last night," she explained. "Michael's horse won and there was no more interest in Deauville or Trouville and as I must buy some things I came on here as soon as I could. I thought I saw you in Cartier's," she explained, "and tried to make you see me when you came out, but only Mr. Denby looked my way so I dared not make any signs of welcome."

She seemed exceedingly happy to be in Paris again, and Denby, looking at her with interest, knew he was in the company of one of the most notable and best liked of the smart hostesses among the sporting set on Long Island. The Harringtons were enormously rich and lived at a great estate near Westbury, not far from the Meadow Brook Club. The Directory of Directors showed the name of Michael Harrington in a number of influential companies, but of recent years his interest in business had slackened and he was more interested in the development of his estate and the training of his thoroughbreds than in Wall Street activities.

For her part she took him, although the name was totally unfamiliar, as a friend of Monty's, and was prepared to like him. Whereas an Englishwoman of her class might have been insistent to discover whether any of his immediate ancestors had been engaged in retail trade before she accepted him as an equal, Alice Harrington was willing to take people on their face value and retain them on their merits.

She saw a tall, well-bred man with strong features and that air of *savoir faire* which is not easy of assumption. She felt instantly that he was the sort of man Michael would like. He talked about racing as though he knew, and that alone would please her husband.

"I've spent so much money," she said presently, "that I shall dismiss this taxi-man and walk. One can walk in Paris with two men, whereas one may be a little pestered alone."

"Fine," Monty cried. "We'll go and lunch somewhere. What place strikes your fancy?"

"Alas," she said, "I'm booked already. I have an elderly relation in the Boulevard Haussmann who stays here all summer this year on account of alterations in the house which she superintends personally, and I've promised."

"I hope she hasn't sacrificed you at a dinner table, too," Denby said, "because if you are free to-night you'd confer a blessing on a fellow countryman if you'd come with Monty and me to the Ambassadeurs. Polin is funnier than ever."

"I'd love to," she cried. "You have probably delivered me from my aunt's dismal dinner. I hadn't an engagement but now I can swear to one truthfully. Men are usually so vain that if you say you're dreadfully sorry but you've another engagement they really believe it. The dear things think no other cause would make a woman refuse. But my aunt would interrogate me till I faltered and contradicted myself."

They left her later at one of those great mansions in the Boulevard Haussmann. The house was enlaced with scaffolding and workmen swarmed over its roof.

"It's old Miss Woodwarde's house," Monty explained. "She's worth millions and will probably leave it to Alice, who doesn't need any, because she's the only one of all her relatives who speaks the truth and doesn't fawn and flatter."

"It takes greater strength of mind than poor relations usually have, to tell rich relatives the truth," Steven reminded him.

Monty had evidently recovered his good spirits. "I knew you'd like her," he said later, "and I knew she'd take to you. We'll have a corking dinner and a jolly good time."

"There's one thing I want to ask of you," Denby said gravely. "Don't give any particulars about me. If she's the sort I think her she won't ask, but you've got a bad habit of wanting people to hear how I fished you out of the river. I want to slip into New York without any advertisement of the fact. I'm not the son of a plutocrat as you are. I'm the hard-up son of a man who was once rich but is now dead and forgotten."

"Do hard-up men hand a million francs across for a string of pearls to put in their tobacco-pouches?" Monty demanded shrewdly.

"You may regard that as an investment if you like," Denby answered. "It may be all my capital is tied up in it."

"You're gambling for a big stake then," Monty said seriously. "Is it worth it, old man?"

For a moment he had an idea of offering him a position in some of the great corporations in which his father was interested, but refrained. Steven Denby was not the kind of man to brook anything that smacked of patronage and he feared his offer might do that although otherwise meant.

"It means a whole lot more to me than you can think," Denby returned. "I have made up my mind to do it and I think I can get away with it in just the way I have mapped out." Then, with a smile: "Monty, I've a proper respect for your imaginative genius, but I'd bet you the necklace to the tobacco-pouch that you don't understand how much I want to get that string of pearls through the customs."

"The pouch is yours," Monty conceded generously. "How should I guess? How do I know who's a smuggler or who isn't? Alice says she always gets something through and for all I know may have a ruby taken from the eye of a Hindoo god in her back hair!"

He looked at his friend eagerly, a new thought striking him. He often surprised himself in romantic ideas, ideas for which Nora was responsible.

"Perhaps you are taking it for someone, someone you're fond of," he suggested.

"Why not?" Denby returned. "If I were really fond of any woman I'd risk more than that to please her."

Monty noticed that he banished the subject by speaking of Alice Harrington's *penchant* for smuggling.

"I hope Mrs. Harrington won't run any risks," he said. "In her case it is absolutely senseless and unnecessary."

"Oh, they'd never get after her," Monty declared. "She's too big. They get after the little fellows but they'd leave Mrs. Michael Harrington alone."

"Don't you believe it," his friend answered. "They're doing things differently now. They're getting a different class of men in the Collector's office."

"I suppose you'd like the old style better," Monty observed.

"Oh, I don't know," said the other. "It's more risky now and so one has to be cleverer. I've often heard it said the hounds have all the fun and the fox none."

"I'm not so sure of that, Monty; I think a fox that can fool thirty couple of hounds and get back to his earth ought to be a gladsome animal."

"I'll find out when we're in West Street, New York," Monty said grimly. "I'll take particular notice of how this fox acts and where the hounds are. If you harp on this any more I shall lose my appetite. What about Voisin's?"

"Eat lightly," Denby counseled him. "I'm going to treat you to a remarkable meal to-night; I know the chef at the Ambassadeurs, and the wine-steward feeds out of my hand."

"I don't see why you shouldn't buy necklaces like that if you have those Ambassadeurs waiters corralled. They soaked me six francs for a single peach once," Monty said reminiscently. But he wondered, all the same, how it was Steven should be able to fling money away as he chose.

His friend looked at him shrewdly. "You're thinking I ought to patronize the excellent Duval," he observed. "Well, sometimes I do. I think I've patronized most places in Paris once."

"Steve, you're a mystery," Monty asserted.

"I hope I am," said the other; "I make my living out of being just that."

They walked in silence to the Rue St. Honoré, Monty still a bit uneasy at being in a crowded place with a friend in whose pocket was a million francs' worth of precious stones. Once or twice as the pocket gaped open he caught a glimpse of the worn pigskin pouch. Steven was taking wholly unnecessary risks, he thought.

As they were leaving Voisin's together after their luncheon it happened that Monty walked behind his friend through the door. Deftly he inserted his hand into the gaping pocket and removed the pouch to his own. He chuckled to think of the object lesson he would presently dilate upon.

When they were near one of those convenient seats which Paris provides for her street-living populace Monty suggested a minute's rest.

With an elaborate gesture he took out the pouch and showed it to Denby.

"Did you ever see this before?" he demanded.

"I've got one just like it," his friend returned without undue interest. "Useful things, aren't they, and last so much longer than the rubber ones?"

"My pouch," said Monty, beginning to enjoy his own joke, "looks better inside than outside. I keep in it tobacco I grow in my private orchid house. Look!"

He pulled back the flap and held it out to Denby.

Denby gazed in it obediently with no change of countenance.

"You're not a heavy smoker, are you?" he returned.

Instantly Monty gazed into it. It was empty except for a shred of tobacco.

"Good God!" he cried. "They've been stolen from me and they put the pouch back!"

"What has?" the other exclaimed.

"The pearls," Monty groaned. "I took them for a joke, and now they're gone!"

He looked apprehensively at Steven, meditating meanwhile how quickly he could turn certain scrip he held into ready money.

Steven evinced no surprise. Instead he rose from his seat and placed a foot upon it as though engaged in tying a lace. But he pointed to the cuff on the bottom of the trouser leg that was on the seat by Monty's side. And Monty, gazing as he was bid, saw his friend's slender fingers pick therefrom a string of pearls.

"I know no safer place," Denby commented judicially. "Of course the customs fellows are on to it, but no pickpocket who ever lived can get anything away from you if you cache it there. On board ship I shall carry it in my pocket, but this is the best place in Paris when one is in strange company."

Monty said no word. His relief was too great and he felt weak and helpless.

"What's the matter?" Denby demanded.

"I want a drink," Monty returned, "but it isn't on you."

CHAPTER THREE

THERE are still restaurants in Paris where a well chosen dinner delights the chef who is called upon to cook it and the waiters who serve. And although it is true that most of the diners of to-day know little of that art which is now disappearing, it happened that Steven Denby was one who delighted the heart of the Ambassadeurs' chef.

Monty was a happy soul who had never been compelled to consult his pocketbook in a choice of restaurants, and Mrs. Michael Harrington was married to a gourmand who well distinguished the difference between that and the indefensible fault of gluttony. Thus both of Denby's guests were in a sense critical. They admitted that they had dined with one who agreed with Dumas' dictum that a dinner is a daily and capital action that can only worthily be accomplished by *gens d'esprit*.

There are few places in Paris where a dinner in summer can be more pleasantly eaten than the balcony at the Ambassadeurs, among slim pillars of palest green and banks of pink roses. In the distance—not too near to be disturbed by the performers unless they chose—the three Americans saw that idol of the place, the great Polin at his best. French waiters do not bring courses on quickly with the idea of using the table a second time during the dining-hour. The financial genius who calculates *l'addition* knows a trick worth two of that.

Still a little anxious that Denby might not be able to stand the expense, Monty fell to thinking of the charges that Parisian restaurateurs can make. "They soaked me six francs for a peach here once," he said for the second time that day.

"That's nothing to what Bignon used to charge," Alice Harrington returned. "Once when Michael's father was dining there he was charged fifteen francs. When he said they must be very scarce in Paris, Bignon said it wasn't the peaches that were scarce, it was the Harringtons."

"Good old Michael," said Monty, "I wish he were here. Why isn't he?"

"Something is being reorganized and the other people want his advice." She laughed. "I suppose he is really good at that sort of thing, but he gets so hopelessly muddled over small accounts that I can't believe it. He was fearfully sorry not to have seen his colt run at Deauville. I shall have to tell him all about it."

"I read the account," said Denby. "St. Mervyn was the name, wasn't it?"

She nodded. "He won by a short head. Michael always likes to beat French horses. I'm afraid he isn't as fond of the country as I am. The only thing he really likes here is the *heure de l'aperitif*. He declares it lasts from four-thirty till seven." She laughed. "He has carried the habit home with him."

"Did you win anything?" Denby asked.

"Enough to buy some presents at Cartier's," she returned. "I've bought something very sweet for Nora Rutledge," she said, turning to Monty. "Aren't you curious to know what? It's a pearl la vallière."

"Then for Heaven's sake, declare it!" Monty cried.

"Oh, no," she said, "I'll pay if it's found, but it's a sporting risk to take and you can't make me believe smuggling's wrong. Michael says it's a Democratic device to rob Republican women."

"Ask Mr. Denby," Monty retorted. "He knows."

"And what do you know, Mr. Denby?" she demanded.

"That the customs people and the state department see no humor in that sort of a joke any longer. You read surely that society women even have been imprisoned for taking sporting risks?"

"Milliners who make a practice of getting things through on their annual trip," she said lightly. "Of course one wouldn't make a business of it, but I've always smuggled little things through and I always shall."

"Well, I wouldn't if I were you," said Monty. "Mr. Denby has frightened me."

Alice Harrington looked at him curiously.

"Have you been caught?" she asked with a smile.

"I've seen others caught," he returned, "and if any sister of mine had to suffer as they did by the publicity and the investigation the customs people are empowered and required to make, I should feel rather uncomfortable."

"What a depressing person you are," she laughed. "I had already decided where to hide the things. I think I shall do it after all. It's been all right before, so why not now?"

He shrugged his shoulders. "It may be the new brooms are sweeping clean or it may be the state department has said smuggling shall no longer be condoned. I only know that things are done very differently now."

Monty looked at him in amazement. His expression plainly meant that he considered his friend the proprietor of an unusually large supply of sheer gall.

"I heard about that," she said, "but one can't believe it. There's a mythical being known only by his initials who is investigating for the state department.

Even Michael warned me, so he may have some inside tip. Have you heard of him, Mr. Denby?"

"I was thinking of him," he answered. "I think they call him R. B. or R. D. or some non-committal thing like that."

"And you believe in him?" she asked sceptically.

"I'm afraid I do," he returned.

"The deuce you do!" Monty cried, aggrieved. He had been happy for the last few hours in the belief that his friend was too well armed to get detected, and here he was admitting, in a manner that plainly showed apprehension, that this initialed power might be even on his track.

"You never smuggle," Alice Harrington said, smiling. "You haven't the nerve, Monty, so you need not take it to heart."

"But I do nevertheless," he retorted.

"Monty," she cried, "I believe you're planning to smuggle something yourself! We'll conspire together and defeat that abominable law."

"If you must," Denby said, still gravely, "don't advertise the fact. Paris has many spies who reap the reward of overhearing just such confidences."

"Spies!" She laughed. "How melodramatic, Mr. Denby."

"But I mean it," he insisted. "Not highly paid government agents, but perhaps such people as chambermaids in your hotel, or servants to whom you pay no attention whatsoever. How do you and I know for example that Monty isn't high up in the secret service?"

"Me?" cried Monty. "Well, I certainly admire your brand of nerve, Steve!"

"That's no answer," his friend returned. "You say you have been two years here studying Continental banking systems. I'll bet you didn't even know that the Banque de France issued a ten thousand franc note!"

"Of course I did," Monty cried, a little nettled.

Denby turned to Mrs. Harrington with an air of triumph.

"That settles it, Monty is a spy."

"I don't see how that proves it," she answered.

"The Banque de France has no ten thousand franc note," he returned; "its highest value is five thousand francs. In two years Montague Vaughan has not found that out. The ordinary tourist who passes a week here and spends nothing to speak of might be excused, but not a serious student like Monty."

"I will vouch for him," Mrs. Harrington said. "I've known him for years and I don't think it's a life suited to him at all, is it, Monty?"

"Oh, I don't know," said he airily. "I may be leading a double life." He looked at her not without an expression of triumph. Little did she know in what a conspiracy he was already enlisted. After an excellent repast and a judicious indulgence in some rare wine Monty felt he was extraordinarily well fitted for delicate intrigue, preferably of an international character. He stroked his budding moustache with the air of a gentleman adventurer.

Alice Harrington smiled. She was a good judge of character and Monty was too well known to her to lend color to any such notion.

"It won't do," she averred, "but Mr. Denby has every earmark of it. There's that piercing look of his and the obsequious way waiters attend on him."

Monty laughed heartily. He was in possession of a secret that made such an idea wholly preposterous. Here was a man with a million-franc pearl necklace in his pocket, a treasure he calmly proposed to smuggle in against the laws of his country, being taken for a spy.

"Alice," he said still laughing, "I'll go bail on Steve for any amount you care to name. I am also willing to back him against all comers for brazen nerve and sheer gall."

Denby interrupted him a little hastily.

"As we two men are free from suspicion, only Mrs. Harrington remains uncleared."

"This is all crazy talk," Monty asserted.

"I know one woman, well known in New York, who goes over each year and more than once has made her expenses by tipping off the authorities to things other women were trying to get through without declaration."

"You speak with feeling," Mrs. Harrington said, and wondered if this friend of Monty's had not been betrayed by some such confidence.

"Are you going to take warning?" Denby asked.

She shook her head. "I don't think so. You've been reading the American papers and are deceived by the annual warnings to intending European tourists. I'm a hardened and successful criminal." She leaned forward to look at a dancer on the stage below them and Denby knew that his monitions had left her unmoved.

"When were you last at home?" she demanded presently of Denby.

"About six months ago," he answered. "I shall be there a week from to-morrow if I live."

The last three words vaguely disturbed Monty. Why, he wondered crossly, was Denby always reminding him of danger? There was no doubt that what his friend really should have said was: "If I am not murdered by criminals for the two hundred thousand dollars' worth of valuables they probably know I carry with me."

"Have you booked your passage yet?" she asked.

It occurred to her that it would be pleasant to have a second man on the voyage. Like all women of her world, she was used to the attentions of men and found life deplorably dull without them, although she was not a flirt and was still in love with her husband.

"Not yet," he answered, "but La Provence goes from Havre to-morrow."

"Come with us," she insisted. "The Mauretania sails a couple of days later but gets you in on the same morning as the other." She turned to Monty. "Isn't that a brilliant idea?"

"It's so brilliant I'm blinded by it," he retorted, gazing at his friend with a look of respect. Not many hours ago Steven had asserted that he and Monty must sail together on the fastest of ships, and now he had apparently decided to forsake the Compagnie Transatlantique only on account of Alice Harrington's invitation.

"I shall be charmed," was all he had said.

Monty felt that he was a co-conspirator of one who was not likely to be upset by trifles. He sighed. A day or so ago he had imagined himself ill-used by Fate because no unusual excitement had come his way, and now his prayers had been answered too abundantly. The phrase "If I live" remained in his memory with unpleasant insistency.

"We ought to cross the Channel by the afternoon boat to-morrow," Alice said. "There are one or two things I want to get for Michael in London."

"It will be a much nicer voyage for me than if I had gone alone on La Provence," Denby said gratefully, while Monty continued to meditate on the duplicity of his sex.

When they had taken Mrs. Harrington to her hotel Monty burst out with what he had been compelled to keep secret all the evening.

"What in thunder makes you so careful about people smuggling?" he demanded.

"About other people smuggling, you mean," Denby corrected.

"It's the same thing," Monty asserted.

"Far from it," his friend made answer. "If Mrs. Harrington is suspected and undeclared stuff found on her, you and I as her companions will be more or less under suspicion too. It is not unusual for women to ask their men friends to put some little package in their pockets till the customs have been passed. The inspectors may have an idea that she has done this with us. Personally I don't relish a very exhaustive search."

"You bet you don't," his friend returned. "I shall probably be the only honest man aboard."

"Mrs. Harrington may ask you to hold some small parcel till she's been through the ordeal," Denby reminded him. "If she does, Monty, you'll be caught for a certainty."

"Damn it all!" Monty cried petulantly, "why can't you people do the right thing and declare what you bring in, just as I do?"

"What is your income?" Denby inquired. "Your father was always liberal with you."

"You mean I have no temptation?" Monty answered. "I forgot that part of it. I don't know what I'd do if there wasn't always a convenient paying teller who passed me out all the currency I wanted."

He looked at his friend curiously, wondering just what this act of smuggling meant to him. Perhaps Denby sensed this.

"You probably wondered why I wrung that invitation out of Mrs. Harrington instead of being honest and saying I, too, was going by the Cunard line. I can't tell you now, Monty, old man, but I hope some day if I'm successful that I can. I tell you this much, though, that it seems so much to me that no little conventionalities are going to stand in my way."

Monty, pondering on this later when he was in his hotel room, called to mind the rumor he had heard years ago that Steven's father had died deeply in debt. It was for this reason that the boy was suddenly withdrawn from Groton. It might be that his struggles to make a living had driven him into regarding the laws against smuggling as arbitrary and inequitable just as Alice Harrington and dozens of other people he knew did. Denby, he argued, had paid good money for the pearls and they belonged to him absolutely; and if by his skill he could evade the payment of duty upon them and sell them at a profit, why shouldn't he? Before slumber sealed his eyes, Montague Vaughan had decided that smuggling was as legitimate a sport as fly-fishing. That these views would shock his father he knew. But his father always prided himself upon a traditional conservatism.

CHAPTER FOUR

LESS than an hour before the Mauretania reached Quarantine, James Duncan, whose rank was that of Customs Inspector and present assignment the more important one of assistant to Daniel Taylor, a Deputy-Surveyor, threw away the stub of cigar and reached for the telephone.

When central had given him his number he called out: "Is that you, Ford?" Apparently the central had not erred and his face took on a look of intentness as he gave the man at the other end of the line his instructions. "Say, Ford," he called, "I've got something mighty important for you. Directly the Mauretania gets into Quarantine, go through the declarations and 'phone me right away whether a man named Steven Denby declares a pearl necklace valued at two hundred thousand dollars. No. No, not that name, Denby, D-E-N-B-Y. Steven Denby. That's right. A big case you say? I should bet it is a big case. Never you mind who's handling it, Ford. It may be R. J., or it may not. Don't you worry about a little thing like that. It's your job to 'phone me as soon as you get a peek at those declarations. Let Hammett work with you. Bye-bye."

He hung up the receiver and leaned back in his chair, well satisfied with himself. He was a spare, hatchet-faced man, who held down his present position because he was used to those storm warnings he could see on his chief's face and knew enough to work in the dark and never ask for explanations.

He did not, for instance, lean back in his chair and smoke cigars with a lordly air when Deputy-Surveyor Daniel Taylor was sitting in his big desk in the window opposite. At such times Duncan worked with silent fury and felt he had evened up matters when he found a Customs Inspector whom he could impress with his own superiority.

When a step in the outside passage warned him that his chief might possibly be coming in, he settled down in an attitude of work. But there entered only Harry Gibbs, dressed in the uniform of a Customs Inspector. Gibbs was a fat, easy man, whose existence was all the more pleasant because of his eager interest in gossip. None knew so well as Gibbs the undercurrent of speculation which the lesser lights of the Customs term office politics. If the Collector frowned, Gibbs instantly dismissed the men upon whom his displeasure had fallen and conjured up erroneous reasons concerning high official wrath. Since Duncan was near to a man in power, Gibbs welcomed any opportunity to converse with him. He seldom came away from such an interview empty-handed. He was a pleasant enough creature and filled with mild wonder at the vagaries of Providence.

Just now he seemed hot but that was not unusual, for he was rarely comfortable during the summer months as he complained frequently. He seemed worried, Duncan thought.

"Hello, Jim," he said when he entered.

Duncan assumed the inquisitorial air his chief had in a marked degree.

"Thought you were searching tourists on the Olympic this afternoon," he replied.

Gibbs mopped his perspiring head, "I was," he answered. "I had two thousand crazy women, all of 'em swearing they hadn't brought in a thing. Gosh! Women is liars."

"What are you doing over here?" Duncan asked.

"I brought along a dame they want your boss Taylor to look over. It needs a smart guy like him to land her. Where is he?"

"Down with Malone now; he'll be back soon."

Gibbs sank into a chair with a sigh of relief. "He don't have to hurry on my account. I'll be tickled to stay here all day. I'm sick of searching trunks that's got nothing in 'em but clothes. It ain't like the good old days, Jim. In them times if you treated a tourist right he'd hand you his business card, and when you showed up in his office next day, he'd come across without a squeal. I used to know the down-town business section pretty well in them days."

"So did I. Why, when I was inspector, if you had any luck picking out your passenger you'd find twenty dollars lying right on the top tray of the first trunk he opened up for you."

Gibbs sighed again. It seemed the golden age was passing.

"And believe me," he said, "when that happened to me I never opened any more of his trunks, I just labeled the whole bunch. But now—why, since this new administration got in I'm so honest it's pitiful."

Duncan nodded acquiescence.

"It's a hell of a thing when a government official has to live on his salary," he said regretfully. "They didn't ought to expect it of us."

"What do they care?" Gibbs asserted bitterly, and then added with that inquiring air which had frequently been mistaken for intelligence: "Ain't it funny that it's always women who smuggle? They'll look you right in the eye and lie like the very devil, and if you do land 'em they ain't ashamed, only sore!"

Duncan assumed his most superior air.

"I guess men are honester than women, Jim, and that's the whole secret."

"They certainly are about smuggling," the other returned. "Why, we grabbed one of these here rich society women this morning and pulled out about forty yards of old lace—and say, where do you think she had it stowed?"

"Sewed it round her petticoat," Duncan said with a grin. He had had experience.

Gibbs shook his head, "No. It was in a hot-water bottle. That was a new one on me. Well, when we pinched her she just turned on me as cool as you please: 'You've got me now, but damn you, I've fooled you lots of times before!'"

Gibbs leaned back in enjoyment of his own imitation of the society lady's voice and watched Duncan looking over some declaration papers. Duncan looked up with a smile. "Say, here's another new one. Declaration from a college professor who paid duty on spending seventy-five francs to have his shoes half-soled in Paris."

But Gibbs was not to be outdone.

"That's nothing," said he, "a gink this morning declared a gold tooth. I didn't know how to classify it so I just told him nobody'd know if he'd keep his mouth shut. It was a back tooth. He did slip me a cigar, but women who are smugglin' seem to think it ain't honest to give an inspector any kind of tip." Gibbs dived into an inner pocket and brought out a bunch of aigrettes. "The most I can do now is these aigrettes. I nipped 'em off of a lady coming down the gangplank of the Olympic. They ain't bad, Jim."

Duncan rose from his chair and came over to Gibbs' side and took the plume from his hand.

"Can't you guys ever get out of the habit of grafting?" he demanded. "Queer," he continued, looking at the delicate feathers closely, "how some soft, timid little bit of a woman is willing to wear things like that. Do you know where they come from?"

"From some factory, I s'pose," Gibbs answered with an air of candor.

"No they don't," Duncan told him. "They take 'em from the mother bird just when she's had her young ones; they leave her half dead with the little ones starving. Pretty tough, I call it, on dumb animals," he concluded, with so sentimental a tone as to leave poor Gibbs amazed. He was still more amazed when his fellow inspector put them in his own pocket and went back to his desk.

"Say, Jim," Gibbs expostulated, "what are you doing with them?"

"Why, my wife was asking this morning if I couldn't get her a bunch. These'll come in just right."

"You're a funny guy to talk about grafting," Gibbs grumbled, "I ain't showing you nothin' more."

"Never you mind me," Duncan commanded. "You keep your own eyes peeled. Old man Taylor's been raising the deuce around here about reports that some of you fellows still take tips."

Gibbs had heard such rumors too often for them to affect him now. "Oh, it's just the usual August holler," he declared.

Duncan contradicted him, "No, it isn't," he observed. "It's because the Collector and the Secretary of the Treasury have started an investigation about who's getting the rake-off for allowing stuff to slip through. I heard the Secretary was coming over here to-day. You keep your eyes peeled, Harry."

"If times don't change," Gibbs said with an air of gloom, "I'm going into the police department."

He turned about to see if the steps he heard at the door were those of the man he had come to see. He breathed relief when he saw it was only Peter, the doorkeeper.

"Mr. Duncan," said the man, "Miss Ethel Cartwright has just 'phoned that she's on her way and would be here in fifteen minutes."

Gibbs looked from one to the other with his accustomed mild interest. He could see that the news of which he could make little had excited Duncan. It was evidently something important. Directly the doorkeeper had gone Duncan called his chief on the telephone and Gibbs sauntered nearer the 'phone. To hear both sides of the conversation would make it much easier.

"Got a cigar, Jim?" he inquired casually of the other, who was holding the wire.

"Yes," said Duncan, taking one from his pocket.

Gibbs reached a fat hand over for it, "Thanks," he returned simply.

Duncan bit the end off and put it in his own mouth. "And I'm going to smoke it myself," he observed.

Gibbs shook his head reprovingly at this want of generosity and took a cigar from his own pocket. "All right then; I'll have to smoke one of my own."

Just then Duncan began to speak over the wire. "Hello. Hello, Chief. Miss Ethel Cartwright just 'phoned she'd be here in fifteen minutes.... Yes, sir.... I'll have her wait."

When he had rung off, Gibbs could see his interest was increasing. "What do you think of her falling for a bum stall like that?"

"Who?" Gibbs demanded. "Which? What stall?"

"Why, Miss Cartwright!" said Duncan. "Ain't I talking about her?"

"Well, who is she?" the aggrieved Gibbs cried. "Is she a smuggler?"

"No. She's a swell society girl," said Duncan in a superior manner.

"If she ain't a smuggler, what's she here for then?" Gibbs had a gentle pertinacity in sticking to his point.

"The Chief wants to use her in the Denby case, so he had me write her a letter saying we'd received a package from Paris containing dutiable goods, a diamond ring, and would she kindly call this afternoon and straighten out the matter." Duncan now assumed an air of triumph. "And she fell for a fake like that!"

"I get you," said Gibbs. "But what does he want her for?"

"I told you, the Denby case."

"What's that?" Gibbs entreated.

Duncan lowered his voice. "The biggest smuggling job Taylor ever handled."

"You don't say so," Gibbs returned, duly impressed. "Why, nobody's told me anything about it."

"Can you keep your mouth shut?" Duncan inquired mysteriously.

"Sure," Gibbs declared. "I ain't married."

"Then just take a peek out of the door, will you?" Duncan directed.

The other did as he was bid. "It's all right," he declared, finding the corridor empty.

"I never know when he may stop out there and listen to what I'm saying. You can hear pretty plain."

"He is the original pussy-foot, ain't he," Gibbs returned. He had known of Taylor's reputation for finding out what was going on in his office by any method. "Now, what's it all about?"

Duncan grew very confidential.

"Last week the Chief got a cable from Harlow, a salesman in Cartier's."

"What's Cartier's?" Gibbs inquired.

"The biggest jewelry shop in Paris. Harlow's our secret agent there. His cable said that an American named Steven Denby had bought a pearl necklace there for a million francs. That's two hundred thousand dollars."

"Gee!" Gibbs cried, duly impressed by such a sum, "But who's Steven Denby? Some new millionaire? I never heard of him."

"Neither did I," Duncan told him; "and we can't find out anything about him and that's what makes us so suspicious. You ought to be able to get some dope on a man who can fling two hundred thousand dollars away on a string of pearls."

Gibbs' professional interest was aroused. "Did he slip it by the Customs, then?"

"He hasn't landed yet," Duncan answered. "He's on the Mauretania."

"Why, she's about due," Gibbs cried.

"I know," Duncan retorted, "I've just had Ford on the 'phone about it. This fellow Denby is traveling with Montague Vaughan—son of the big banker—and Mrs. Michael Harrington."

"You mean *the* Mrs. Michael Harrington?" Gibbs demanded eagerly.

"Sure," Duncan exclaimed, "there's only one."

Gibbs was plainly disappointed at this ending to the story.

"If he's a friend of Mrs. Harrington and young Vaughan, he ain't no smuggler. He'll declare the necklace."

"The Chief has a hunch he won't," Duncan said. "He thinks this Denby is some slick confidence guy who has wormed his way into the Harringtons' confidence so he won't be suspected."

Gibbs considered the situation for a moment.

"Maybe he ain't traveling with the party at all but just picked 'em up on the boat."

Duncan shook his head. "No, he's a friend all right. She's taking him down to the Harrington place at Westbury direct from the dock. One of the stewards on the Mauretania is our agent and he sent us a copy of her wireless to old man Harrington."

"He sounds to me like a sort of smart-set Raffles," Gibbs asserted.

"You've got it right," Duncan said approvingly.

"What's Taylor going to do?" Gibbs asked next.

"He's kind of up against it," Duncan returned. "I don't know what he'll do yet. If Denby's on the level and we pinch him and search him and don't find anything, think of the roar that Michael Harrington—and he's worth about ninety billion—will put up at Washington because we frisked one of his pals. Why, he'd go down there and kick to his swell friends and we'd all be fired."

"I ain't in on it," Gibbs said firmly; "they've no cause to fire me. But how does this Miss Cartwright come in on the job?"

"I don't know except that she is going down to the Harringtons' this afternoon and Taylor's got some scheme on hand. I tell you he's a pretty smart boy."

"You bet he is," Gibbs returned promptly, "and may be he's smarter than you know. Ever hear of R. J.?"

"R. J.?" Duncan repeated. "You mean that secret service agent?"

"Yes," Gibbs told him with an air of one knowing secret things. "They say he's a pal of the President's."

"Well, what's that to do with this?" Duncan wanted to know.

"Don't you know who he is?"

"No," Duncan retorted, "and neither does anyone else. Nobody but the President and the Secretary of the Treasury knows who he really is."

Gibbs rose from his chair and patted his chest proudly. "Well, I know, too," he declared.

Duncan laughed contemptuously. "Yes, you do, just the same as I do—that he's the biggest man in the secret service, and that's all you know."

Gibbs smiled complacently. "Ain't it funny," he observed, "that you right here in the office don't know?"

"Don't know what?" Duncan retorted sharply; he disliked Gibbs in a patronizing rôle.

"That your boss Taylor is R. J."

"Taylor!" Duncan cried. "You're crazy! The heat's got you, Harry."

"Oh, indeed!" Gibbs said sarcastically. "Do you remember the Stuyvesant case?"

Duncan nodded.

"And do you remember that when Taylor took his vacation last year R. J. did some great work in the Crosby case? Put two and two together, Jim, and may be you'll see daylight."

"By George!" Duncan exclaimed, now impressed by Gibbs' news. "I believe you're right. Taylor never will speak about this R. J., now I come to think of it." He raised his head as the sound of voices was heard in the passage.

"There he is," Duncan whispered busying himself with a sheaf of declarations.

Gibbs looked toward the opening door nervously. It was one thing to criticize the deputy-surveyor in his absence and another to meet his look and endure his satire. His collar seemed suddenly too small, and he chewed his cigar violently.

CHAPTER FIVE

DANIEL TAYLOR entered quickly without acknowledging the presence of his inferiors and crossed to his desk by the window. He was a man above medium height, broad of shoulder, thick through the chest and giving the idea of one who was alert and aggressive mentally and physically. Those in the service who had set themselves against him had been broken. His path had been strewn with other men's regrets; but Taylor climbed steadily, never caring for what was below, but grasping eagerly for power.

Naturally a man of his type must have had other qualities than mere aggressiveness to aid him in such vigorous competition. He had commended himself to the powers above him for snap judgment and quick action. And although men of his temperament must inevitably make mistakes, it was notorious that Taylor made fewer than his rivals.

Toward men like Duncan and Gibbs who were not destined to rise, men who could be replaced without trouble, Taylor paid small heed. They did what he told them and if they failed he never forgot. It was to the men above him that Taylor showed what small social gifts nature had given him. He had sworn to rise in the service and he cultivated only those who might aid him.

After glancing over the papers arranged on his desk he called to Duncan: "Has Miss Cartwright been here yet?"

"No, sir," Duncan responded promptly.

His superior pushed the buzzer on his desk and then looked across at the uncomfortable Gibbs. "Want to see me?" he snapped.

"Yes, sir," Gibbs made answer as Peter the doorkeeper entered in answer to Taylor's summons.

"Then wait outside," Taylor said, "I'll see you in five minutes."

"Yes, sir," Gibbs said obediently and made his exit.

The deputy-surveyor turned toward the attendant. "Peter, let me know the instant Miss Cartwright arrives. Don't forget; it's important. That's all."

He dismissed Peter with a nod and then called to Duncan.

"Did Bronson of the New York Burglar Insurance Company send over some papers to me relating to the theft of Miss Cartwright's jewels?"

Duncan took a long envelope and laid it on his chief's desk. "Here they are, sir."

Taylor looked at the documents eagerly. "By George!" he cried, when he had looked into them, "I knew I was right. I knew there was something queer about the way her diamonds were stolen."

Duncan looked at him frowning. He prided himself upon his grasp of detail and here was the Chief talking about a case he knew naught of. "What diamonds?" he asked. "The case wasn't in our office, was it?"

"No," said Taylor, "this is a little outside job my friend Bronson's mixed up in, but it may be a help to us." He went on reading the papers and presently exclaimed: "It's a frame-up. She wasn't robbed, although she collected from the company on a false claim."

"But I can't see—" the puzzled Duncan returned.

"No," said his chief, cutting him short. "If you could, you'd have my job. Has the Mauretania got to Quarantine yet?"

"Not yet, sir," Duncan answered.

"Telephone Brown to notify you the minute she does. Tell him we've got to know as soon as possible whether Denby declares that necklace; everything depends on that."

"But he may declare it," Duncan observed sagely.

"If he does we haven't a case," his superior said briefly, "but I've a feeling there's not going to be a declaration."

"I think so, too," Duncan asserted, "and I'm holding Ford and Hammett to search him."

Taylor frowned and drummed on the desk with his fingers. "I don't know that I want him searched. Let them do nothing without my instructions."

"But, Chief," Duncan protested, "if he doesn't declare the necklace and you don't have him searched he'll smuggle it in."

"I know, I know," Taylor said impatiently, "but I've got to be cautious how I go about taking liberties with a friend of Michael Harrington's. He has more influence than you've any idea of. We've got to be sure we have the goods on Denby."

Duncan looked at the other with grudging admiration. "Well, I guess it won't take R. J. very long to land him."

Taylor turned on the speaker with a scowl. "What's he got to do with this?"

"I thought you might have interested him in it," Duncan said meaningly.

"I don't know anything about him," Taylor returned.

It was like the Chief to refuse to take his underlings into his confidence, Duncan thought, so he took his cue and changed the subject.

"Well," he said, reverting to the proposed search of Denby, "if we don't go through him at the dock, what are we going to do?"

"Let him slide through easily and think he's fooled us," Taylor said. "He may be pretty clever. Do you remember that man who stuck the sapphire we were hunting for into a big rosy apple he gave to a woman in the second cabin and then took it away from her before she had time to eat it? We'll see if he talks to anyone, but I think he'll take the pearls right down to Westbury. He'll be off his guard when once he gets down there."

"Have you got one of the Harrington servants to spy for us?" Duncan cried.

"I've got what will be better than that with a little luck," Taylor said with a smile. "Don't you know that Miss Ethel Cartwright is going down to Westbury this afternoon to spend the week-end with the Harringtons?"

"You don't mean you're going to use her?" Duncan exclaimed, incredulity in his tone.

"It wouldn't be a bad idea, would it, Jim?"

"It would be a peach of an idea if you could do it, but can you?"

Taylor chuckled. It was plain he had some scheme in his crafty brain that pleased him more than a little.

"I'm going to answer that as soon as I've had a little confidential chat with Miss Cartwright."

He broke off to turn to the doorway through which Gibbs' head protruded.

"Can I see you now, Chief?" Gibbs asked.

"What is it?" Taylor snapped.

"There's a deaf and dumb chicken out here," Gibbs replied anxiously.

"A what?" the other demanded.

"A girl that can't hear or speak or write. They say she's smuggled a bracelet in but they've searched her eight times and can't get a trace of it, so they sent her to you."

"They don't expect me to make the ninth attempt, do they?" the Chief queries.

"Why, no," Gibbs told him, "but they thought you might hand her the third degree."

"Bring her in," the autocrat commanded. When Gibbs had closed the door Taylor turned to Duncan. "She's probably bluffing. Put that chair here. We'll try the gun gag on her. There's a revolver in my second drawer. When I say 'Go,' you shoot. Got it?"

"Yes, sir," Duncan said, anticipating a theatrical scene in which his chief would shine as usual. Duncan always enjoyed such episodes; he felt he shone with reflected power.

Gibbs dragged in a young girl and stood her in front of the chair to which the Chief had beckoned. "Sit down," Gibbs commanded. The afflicted woman who was named, so Gibbs said, Sarah Peabody, remained standing. "Hey, *squattez-vous*," her captor commanded again in a louder voice. Still Sarah was unmoved. Gibbs scratched his head and summoned his linguistic attainments to his aid.

"*Setzen sie*," he shouted, but Miss Peabody remained erect.

Gibbs turned away with a gesture of despairing dignity. "I'm done," he asserted; "that's all the languages I know. I used to think it was a terrible thing that women could talk, but I guess the Almighty knew more than I did."

Duncan essayed more active measures. He pushed her into the seat. "Hey you," cried he, "sit down there."

Gibbs watched a little apprehensively. If Sarah Peabody had been normal, he would have pictured her as a slangy and fluent young woman with a full-sized temper. He had dealt with such before and they invariably defeated him in wordy combat. In duels of this sort Gibbs was slow to get off the mark.

Taylor came toward the afflicted one and looked shrewdly into her face. "She's not shamming," said he. "She's got that stupid look they all have when they're deaf and dumb." He watched her closely as he said this.

"She ain't spoke all day," Gibbs volunteered, "and no woman what could, would keep from talking that long."

"Women will do a lot for diamonds," his chief observed.

"None of 'em ever do me for none," Gibbs remarked placidly.

Suddenly Taylor addressed the girl roughly. "If you're acting," he cried, "you'd better give it up, because I'm certain to find out, and if I do, I'll send you to jail." Still the girl paid no attention but only stared ahead blankly. "So you won't answer, eh?" said her inquisitor. "Going to force my hand, are you?" He raised his hand to signal Duncan and then added: "Go."

The loud report of the revolver, while it made Gibbs jump, had no effect upon the young woman. Taylor shook his head wisely. "I guess she's deaf and dumb all right, poor girl. What's it all about, Gibbs? What is it you think she's done?"

"She's got a bracelet chuck-full of diamonds, and we can't find it."

"How do you know she's got it?" the Chief asked.

"She showed it to a woman who was in the same cabin," Gibbs returned, "and the woman came and tipped us off."

"Why, the dirty hussy!" cried the girl, who had previously been bereft of hearing and speech, rising to her feet, her eyes flashing, and her whole face denoting rage.

Gibbs looked at her, his eyes bulging with startled surprise, and then turned his ox-like gaze upon Taylor.

"For the love of Mike!" said Gibbs at length, but Sarah Peabody cut short any other exclamations.

"Do you know why she told about me?" the girl demanded. "She wanted to alibi herself and make you folks thinks she was an honest God-fearing lady that would never smuggle—and she had four times as much as I did. Why, it was her who put me up to smuggling and taught me to be deaf and dumb." Sarah ground her white teeth in anger. "I'd like to meet her again some time."

"You shall," Taylor cried. "When we arrest her we'll need your evidence to testify against her."

"You can bet I won't be deaf and dumb then," Miss Peabody cried viciously.

"Where's the bracelet?" Taylor snapped. "Don't waste time now."

But the smuggler was no fool and not intimidated by his tones. "Wait a minute," she said craftily. "What's going to happen to me?"

"Produce it, pay the duty, and we'll let you go free for the tip."

"You're on," said Sarah joyously. "Just take a look at the ring handle of my parasol. I've painted over the stones, that's all."

Gibbs grabbed it from her and examined it closely. "Well, can you approach that?" he said helplessly. "And I've been carrying it around all day!"

Taylor turned from his examination of the parasol as Peter the doorkeeper entered. "Miss Cartwright here?" he asked quickly.

"Yes, sir," answered the man. "She's just arrived."

"Bring her in as soon as these get out," Taylor said dismissing him.

"Take her away now, Gibbs," he said, indicating the owner of the magic parasol. "Turn her over to Shorey, he can handle her from now on."

"All right, sir," Gibbs said, still undecided as to why he had been fooled.

Sarah looked at him with scorn. "I'll be glad to have someone else on the job. I'm sick o' trottin' around with a fat guy like him."

"Say, now," Gibbs protested in an injured manner.

But Taylor had a bigger scheme on hand and waved her away impatiently. "Take her along, Gibbs."

She gave Taylor an impudent little nod of farewell. "Ta-ta old Sport. I certainly fooled you, when you had that gun shot off."

Gibbs had grabbed her by the arm and was now pushing her toward the door. "And I could have kept it up," Miss Peabody asserted in a shrill tone, "if it hadn't made me sore, her putting over one on me like that. And she was so blamed nice to me. But when one woman's nice to another she means mischief, you can bet your B. V. D.'s."

Even Taylor smiled as she went. He had nearly met defeat but his habitual luck had made him victor in the end. He hoped it would aid him in a far more difficult interview which was to come.

Duncan took advantage of his good humor to ask a question.

"Do you really think you can get Miss Cartwright to help us on the Denby case?"

He had so often seen her name in the society columns that he doubted if his chief, clever as he was, could successfully influence her.

Taylor looked at him curiously. There was in his eyes a look that spoke of more than a faint hope of success. Few knew better than Duncan of his ability to make men and women his tools.

"Jim," he said with an air of confidence, "I wouldn't be a bit surprised if she offered to help us."

The door opened and Peter entered.

"Miss Ethel Cartwright," he announced.

Taylor rose to his feet as she entered and bowed with what grace he could as he motioned her to a chair.

Miss Cartwright was a tall, strikingly pretty woman of twenty-seven, who looked at the deputy-surveyor with the perfect self-possession which comes so easily to those whose families have long been of the cultured and leisured classes. It was plain that this rather languid young lady regarded him merely as some official whom she was bound to see regarding a matter of business.

"Sorry if I kept you waiting, Miss Cartwright," Taylor said briskly.

"It doesn't matter in the least," she returned graciously. "I've never been at the Customs before. I found it quite interesting."

"My name is Taylor," he said, "and I'm a deputy-surveyor."

"You wanted to see me about a ring, I think, didn't you?"

"Yes," he answered. "The intention evidently was to smuggle it through the Customs."

"Do you really think so?" she demanded, interested. "I haven't the faintest idea who could have sent it to me."

"Of course you haven't," he said in his blandest, most reassuring manner. It was a manner that made the listening Duncan wonder what was to follow. His chief was always most deadly when he purred. "It's a mistake," he continued, "but the record will probably shed some light on the matter. Duncan," he called sharply, "go and get those papers relating to Miss Cartwright."

His assistant looked at him blankly.

"Papers?" he repeated. "What papers, sir?"

"The papers relating to the package sent Miss Cartwright from Paris." There was a significance in his tone that was not lost on Duncan. Gibbs would have argued it out, but Duncan though in the dark followed his cue.

"Oh, *those* papers," he answered. "I'll get 'em, sir."

When he had gone the girl turned to Taylor.

"Do you know," she asserted, "I feel quite excited at being here and sitting in a chair in which you probably often examine smugglers. One reads about it constantly."

"It's being done all the time," he responded, "among all sorts of people. Now, Miss Cartwright, since we are talking of smuggling, I'd like to have a little business chat with you if I may."

The girl looked at him astonished. She could not conceive that a man like the one looking at her could be serious in talking of a business proposition.

"With me?" she demanded, and Taylor could see that the idea was not pleasing. He resolved to abandon his usual hectoring tactics and adopt softer modes.

"I mean it," he asserted. "You said you've read about all this smuggling and so on. Believe me, you've not read a thousandth part of what's going on all the time, despite all our efforts to check it. The difficult part is that many of the women are so socially prominent that it isn't easy to detect them. They move in the sort of world you move in." He leaned forward and spoke impressively. "But it's a world where neither I nor my men could pass muster for a moment. Do you follow me?"

"I hear what you say," she said, "but—"

He interrupted her, "Miss Cartwright, we are looking for someone who belongs in society by right. Someone who is clever enough to provide us with information and yet never be suspected. We want someone above suspicion. We want someone, for instance, like you."

That his proposition was offensive to her he could see from the faint flush that passed over her face and the rather haughty tone that she adopted.

"Really, Mr. Taylor," she cried, "you probably mean well, but—"

Again he cut her short.

"Just listen a moment, Miss Cartwright," he begged. "I have reason to know that your family has been in financial difficulties since your father died." He looked at her shrewdly. "The position I hinted at could be made very profitable. How would you like to enter the secret service of the United States Customs?" He could see she was far from being placated at his hint of financial reward.

"This is quite too preposterous," she said icily. "It may possibly be your idea of a joke, Mr. Taylor, but it is not mine."

"I'm not joking," he cried, "I'm in dead earnest."

"If that's the case," she returned, rising, "I must ask you to get the papers regarding the ring."

"They'll be here at any moment," he answered. "I'm sorry you don't care to entertain my proposition, but it's your business after all. By the way," he added, after a moment's pause, "there's another little matter I'd like to take up with you while we're waiting. Do you recall a George Bronson, the claim agent of the New York Burglar Insurance Company, the company which insured the jewels that were stolen from you?"

"I think I do," she returned slowly, "but—"

"Well, that company has had a great deal of trouble with society women who have got money by pawning their jewels and then putting in a claim that they were stolen and so recovering from the company on the alleged loss."

The girl looked at him, frowning. "Are you trying to insinuate that—"

"Certainly not," Taylor purred amiably. "Why, no. I'm merely explaining that that's what Bronson thought at first, but after investigating, he found out how absurd the idea was."

"Naturally," she said coldly.

She had come into the deputy-surveyor's office with an agreeable curiosity regarding a present sent her from Paris. But the longer she stayed, the less certain did she feel concerning this hard-faced man opposite her, who had the strangest manner and made the most extraordinary propositions. What business was it of his that her jewels had been stolen?

"But there were some things he could not understand," Taylor went on.

"May I ask," she cried, "what Mr. Bronson's inability to understand has to do with you?"

"Simply," said Taylor with an appearance of great frankness, "that he happens to be a very good friend of mine and often consults me about things that puzzle him. The theft of those jewels of yours mystified him greatly."

"Mystified him?" the girl retorted. "It was perfectly simple."

"Perhaps you won't mind telling me the circumstances of the case."

"Really," she returned sub-acidly, "I don't quite understand how this concerns the Customs."

"It doesn't," he agreed readily, "I am acting only as Bronson's friend and if you'll answer my questions I may be able to recover the jewels for you."

The girl's face cleared. So far from acting inimically, Mr. Taylor was actually going to help her. She smiled for the first time, and resumed her seat.

"That will be splendid," she exclaimed. "I did not understand. Of course I'll tell you everything I know."

"The first feature that impressed Bronson," said the deputy-surveyor, "and me, I'm bound to add, was that the theft seemed to be an inside job."

"What does that mean?" Miss Cartwright queried, interested.

"That there was no evidence that a thief had broken into your home."

"But what other explanation could there be?" she inquired. "Our family consists of just my mother, my sister and myself, and two old servants who have lived with us for years, so of course it wasn't any of us."

"Naturally not," Taylor agreed as though this explanation had solved his doubts. "But how did you come to discover the loss of the diamonds?"

"I didn't discover it myself," she told him. "I was at Bar Harbor."

"Oh," said Taylor with the confidential air of a family physician. "You were away. I see! Who did find out?"

"My sister. It was she who missed them."

"Oh, your sister missed them, did she?" he said.

He pushed the buzzer and wrote something on a slip of paper.

"So of course," the girl continued, "it must have been some thief from the outside."

Taylor looked thoughtful. "I suppose you're right," he admitted, and then asked quickly: "I wonder if you'd mind telephoning your sister to come down here now?"

"Why, she came with me," Miss Cartwright returned. "She's outside."

"That's fine," he said brightly. "It makes it easier." He pushed the buzzer again. "Perhaps she'll be able to help us."

"She'll come if I wish," said the elder sister, "but she knows even less about it than I do."

"I understand that," Taylor said smoothly, "but she may remember a few seemingly unimportant details that will help me where they wouldn't seem significant to you."

He looked up as Peter came in. "Ask Miss Cartwright's sister to come in for a moment. Tell her Miss Ethel wants to talk to her."

"Amy will tell you all she can," the girl asserted.

"Just as you would yourself," Taylor said confidentially. He had no other air than of a man who is sworn to recover stolen diamonds. Ethel Cartwright admitted she had misjudged him.

"It must be wonderful to be a detective and piece together little unimportant facts into an important whole."

"It is," he answered a trifle drily; "quite wonderful."

Amy Cartwright was brought into the deputy-surveyor's room by Peter. Plainly she was of a less self-reliant type than her elder sister, for the rather startled expression her face wore was lost when she saw Ethel. She was a pretty girl not more than eighteen and like her sister dressed charmingly.

"You wanted me, Ethel?" she asked.

"Yes, dear," the elder returned. "Amy, this is Mr. Taylor, who thinks he may be able to get back my diamonds for me."

Amy Cartwright shot a quick, almost furtive look at Taylor and then gripped her sister's arm. "Your diamonds!" she cried.

Taylor had missed nothing of her anxious manner. "Yes," he said. "Your sister has been kind enough to give me some information in reference to the theft, and I thought you might be able to add to the facts we already have."

"I?" the younger girl exclaimed.

"Yes," her sister commanded. "You must answer all Mr. Taylor's questions."

"Of course," Amy said with an effort to be cheerful.

Taylor looked at her magisterially. "How did you discover your sister's jewels were stolen?"

"Why," she replied nervously, not meeting his eye, "I went to her dressing-table one morning and they weren't there."

"Oh!" he exclaimed meaningly. "So they weren't there! Then what did you do?"

"Why, I telephoned to the company she insured them in."

"Without consulting your sister?" he asked. His manner, although quick and alert, was friendly. Ethel Cartwright felt he was desirous of helping her, and if Amy seemed nervous, it was her first experience with a man of this type. She had so little experience in relying on herself that this trifling ordeal was magnified into a judicial cross-examination. She determined to help Amy out.

"You must remember," she said to Taylor, "that I was out of town."

"Of course!" Amy exclaimed with a show of relief. "How could I consult her when she was in Maine?"

"Were you certain she hadn't taken her diamonds with her?" he asked.

Amy hesitated for a moment. "I think she must have told me before she left."

"Hm!" he ejaculated. "You *think* she did?"

Amy turned to her sister. "Didn't you tell me, Ethel?"

Miss Cartwright knit her brows in thought. "Perhaps I did," she admitted.

"But you didn't telegraph your sister to make sure?" Taylor queried.

"Why, no," the girl said hesitating and seemingly confused. "No, I didn't." She was now staring at her interrogator with real fear in her eyes.

"Well, that doesn't make any difference," he said genially, "so long as the jewels were stolen and not merely mislaid, does it?"

"No," she said with a sigh of relief.

"There's one other point," he said, turning to the elder sister. "You received the compensation money from the company, didn't you?"

"Naturally," she said tranquilly.

"Please don't think me impertinent," he said, "but you still have it intact, I presume?"

"Only part," the girl returned. "I gave half of it to my sister."

"I rather thought you might have done that," he purred as though his especial hobby was discovering affection in other families, "That was a very nice generous thing to do, Miss Cartwright. But you realize of course that if I get your jewels back the money must be returned to the Burglar Insurance people in full,"—he looked significantly at the shrinking younger girl,—"from both of you."

Amy Cartwright clasped her hands nervously. "Oh, I couldn't do that," she exclaimed.

Ethel turned to her in astonishment.

"But Amy, why not?"

"I haven't got it all now."

"But, dear, what did you do with it?" Ethel persisted.

Taylor seemed to take a keen interest in Amy Cartwright's financial affairs.

"That's quite an interesting question," he observed judiciously. "What did you do with your half?"

"I—I paid a lot of bills," the girl stammered.

"Paid a lot of bills!" her sister exclaimed. "But Amy, you distinctly told me—"

"One minute," Taylor interrupted. "Now, Miss Amy," he said sharply, "what sort of bills did you pay?"

"Oh, dressmakers and hats and things," she answered with a trace of sullenness.

"Of course they gave you receipts?" he suggested.

"I don't remember," she answered.

"Oh, you don't remember," he said, fixing her with his cold eye. "But you remember whom you paid the money to?"

"Of course she does," Ethel cried, coming to her sister's aid. She was herself puzzled at this strange man's attitude. "You do, don't you, Amy?"

"Why, yes," the other said weakly.

"Give me the names!" Taylor demanded, and then looked angrily up to see who had entered his office unbidden. It was James Duncan, apologetic, but urged by powers higher than those of his chief.

"The Collector and the Secretary want to see you right away, sir," he announced.

"I can't leave now," Taylor cried angrily. And in that moment both girls realized of what ruthless metal he was cast. Gone was the amiable interest in family matters and the kindly wish to aid two girls in getting back their trinkets, and there was left a strong remorseless man who showed he had them very nearly in his power.

But Duncan dared not go back with such a message.

"I explained you were busy, Chief," he said, "but they would have you come down at once, as the Secretary has to go back to Washington. It's about that necklace. The one coming in on the Mauretania this afternoon."

"Oh, very well," his superior snapped. "I shall have to ask you ladies to excuse me for five minutes."

"Certainly," Ethel Cartwright returned.

At the door Taylor beckoned to Duncan and spoke in a whisper. "Get outside in the corridor and if they try to leave, stop 'em. And I shall want to know what they've been talking about. Understand?"

"Sure, Chief," Duncan returned.

When both men had gone from the room Amy clung half-hysterically to her strong, calm sister. "Oh, Ethel, they know, they know!"

"Know what?" Ethel asked, amazed at the change in the other.

"That man suspects," Amy whispered. "I know he does. Did you see how he glared at me and the way he spoke?"

"Suspects what?" Ethel asked. "Amy, what do you mean? What is there to suspect?"

"Don't let them take me away!" the younger sister wailed. "Oh, don't, don't!"

Ethel drew back a step and looked into the trembling Amy's tear-stained face.

"What is this you are saying?" she asked sharply.

"Ethel, your jewels weren't stolen." There was a pause as if the girl were trying to gather courage enough to confess. "I took them. I pawned them."

"Amy!" cried the other. "You?"

"I had to have money. I took them. A woman told me I could get it by pretending to the company the things were stolen. She said they'd never find it out and would pay. I tried it, and they paid."

Miss Cartwright looked down at her, amazed, indignant, horrified.

"Do you mean to say you deliberately swindled the company?"

"I couldn't help it, Ethel," she declared piteously. "I didn't think of it in that way. I didn't mean to. I didn't, indeed."

"Why, why, why? Why in God's name did you do it? Tell me quickly, why?"

Amy could no longer meet her sister's glance. She dropped her head.

"I lost a lot of money gambling, playing auction bridge."

"Playing with whom?" Ethel demanded sharply.

"People you don't know," the younger answered evasively. "It was while you were away. It wouldn't have happened if you'd been home. We all dined together at the Claremont and afterwards they simply would play auction. I said no at first but they made me. I got excited and began to lose, and then they said if I kept on the luck would turn, but it didn't, and I lost a thousand dollars."

Ethel Cartwright needed no other explanation as a key to Taylor's manner. It was certain that he knew and would presently force her poor frightened little sister into a confession. It was no time for blaming the child or pointing out morals, but for protecting her.

"Ssh," she whispered, "Ssh!"

"I didn't mean to do it," Amy reiterated. "Believe me, I didn't."

"Tell me what happened then?" Ethel asked in a low tone.

"I couldn't pay, of course, and the other women said they'd have to ask mother or you for the money and if you wouldn't pay I should have to go to jail. I didn't know what to do. I nearly went out of my head, I think. At last Philip Sloane offered to lend it me."

The elder recoiled from her. "That man!" she cried horrified. "Oh, Amy, and how often I have warned you against him!"

"There was nothing else to do," her sister explained. "You were away and I had no one to go and ask."

"Stop a minute," Ethel said. "If you borrowed the money and paid the debts, why did you need to take my diamonds?"

Amy hung her head. "When he lent me the money he said I could pay it back whenever I wanted to, in a hundred years if I liked."

"Well?" Ethel cried anxiously. "Well?"

"But a day or so later he came to see me, mother was out, and his manner was so different I was frightened. He—he said a girl who accepts money from a man is never any good, and nobody will believe them no matter what they say. I didn't think men could be like that. He said he'd forget about it if I went away with him. He said nobody would know it—he could arrange all that—and he threatened all sorts of things. Oh, everything you said about him was right."

"Go on," her sister commanded, in a hard staccato tone. "What then?"

"At first I thought of killing myself but I was afraid. And then I saw your jewel-case and I pretended they were stolen. I got half the money from the pawn-shop and the other half from you when the company settled. It was wicked of me, Ethel, but what could I do?"

Ethel put her arm about the poor sobbing girl very tenderly.

"My poor little sister," she whispered, "my little Amy, you did the better thing after all. But you should have told me before, so that I could have helped you."

"I was afraid to," the girl said, looking into the face above her, "I meant to have told you next month when that money is coming from father's estate. I thought we could pay the company then so that I shouldn't feel like a thief. I'm so glad I've told you; it has frightened me so!" But the grave expression on Ethel's face alarmed her. "Why do you look like that?" she demanded.

"It will be all right," Ethel assured her. "But you know those dividends have been delayed this month and neither mother nor I have any spare money if the Burglar Insurance people want to be paid back. I daresay we can arrange something, so don't be frightened. And remember, this man Taylor can't know certainly. He only suspects, and we ought to be able to beat him if we are very careful. I'm so glad you told me so that I know what to do."

"But I'm afraid of him," Amy cried. "I shall break down and they'll put me in prison. Ethel, I should die if they did that."

"I'll save you, dear," Ethel said comfortingly. "You know you have always been able to believe in me, and I will save you if only you try to control yourself."

"Then let me go home," Amy cried, panic-stricken by the thought of another interview with the resourceful Taylor. "I shall break down if I stay here."

"That will be best," Ethel agreed, and went quickly to the door, behind which she found Duncan on guard.

"Sorry, miss," he said respectfully, "but you can't go."

"I'm not leaving," Ethel Cartwright explained, "I still have to talk with Mr. Taylor, but my sister must go. She isn't feeling very well. She wants to go home."

Duncan shook his head. "Neither of you can go," he returned, as he closed the door. Amy looked about her nervously for other means of escape.

"You see," she whispered, "they're going to keep me here a prisoner! What shall I do?"

"Leave everything to me," Ethel commanded. "Let me do the talking. I shall be able to think of some way out."

"There isn't, there isn't!" Amy moaned.

"Stop crying," the elder insisted. "That won't help us. I've thought of a plan. I'll invent a story to fool him. He won't be able to find out whether it's true or not, so he'll have to let us go, and when he does, he won't get us back here again in a hurry."

"Oh, Ethel, you're wonderful!" Amy exclaimed, her face clearing. In all her small troubles she had always gone to this beautiful, serene elder sister, who had never yet failed her and never would, she was confident.

When Taylor entered a minute later he found the two girls looking out of the big window across the harbor. They seemed untroubled and unafraid and were discussing the dimensions of a big liner making her way out.

"Sorry to have had to leave you," he said briskly, "especially as things were getting a bit interesting."

Ethel Cartwright looked at him coldly. It was a glance which Taylor rightly interpreted as a warning to remember that he occupied a wholly different sphere from that of the daughters of the late Vernon Cartwright. But it daunted him little. The Secretary of the Treasury had just told him that his work was evoking great interest in Washington. And the Collector somewhat cryptically had said that Daniel Taylor might always be relied upon to do the unexpected. For Washington and Collectors, Taylor had little respect.

Unconsciously he often paraphrased that royal boast, "*L'État c'est moi!*" by admitting to his confidants that he, Daniel Taylor, was the United States Customs.

"I quite fail to see," Miss Cartwright observed chillingly, "what all this rather impertinent cross-questioning of my sister has to do with—"

"You will in a minute," he interrupted.

"Meanwhile," she said, "I can't wait any longer for those papers about the ring."

"There isn't any ring," he said suavely. "That was just a pretext to get you here. I was afraid the truth wouldn't be sufficiently luring so I had to employ a ruse."

She looked at him, her eyes flashing at his daring to venture on such a deception. "You actually asked me to come here because you thought I had swindled the company?"

"Well," he observed genially, "we all make our little mistakes."

"So you admit it was a mistake?" she said, hardly knowing what to make of this changed manner.

"I'm quite sure of it," he asserted. "*You* are innocent, Miss Cartwright. How am I so sure of it? Because I happen to have the thief already."

"You have the thief?" Amy cried, startled out of her determination to say nothing.

"Yes," he told her nonchalantly, "I've arrested the man who robbed your sister. Poor devil, he has a wife and children. He swears they'll starve, and very likely they will, but he's guilty and to jail he goes."

"Are you sure he's guilty?" Amy stammered.

He leaned over his desk and looked at her surprised. "Why, yes," he said slowly. "Have you any reason to think different?"

"No, no!" she cried, shrinking back.

"But I have," Ethel said calmly. "I have every reason to believe he is innocent."

"*You* have?" Taylor cried, himself perplexed at the turn things were taking.

Amy looked at her sister, wondering what was coming next.

"I know who stole them," Ethel went on. "It was my maid."

"Your maid!" the deputy-surveyor cried. "Why didn't you tell the company that? Bronson never told me about it."

"She didn't disappear till after the claim was paid, you see," Miss Cartwright explained. "Then I got a note from her confessing, a note written in Canada."

"Whereabouts in Canada?" he demanded.

"I don't recall it," he was told.

"You don't? Well, what was your maid's name then? I'd like to know that, if you can remember it for me."

"Marie Garnier was her name."

He took up a scribbling pad and inscribed the name on it. "Marie Garnier," he muttered, and pushed the buzzer. "Why didn't you tell me this before?"

"What was the good?" Miss Cartwright returned. "I was fond of Marie—she was almost one of the family—and I didn't want to brand her as a thief. When I learned she had escaped to Canada where the law couldn't reach her—"

She was interrupted by Duncan's entrance. "Yes, sir?" said he to his chief.

Taylor handed him the leaf he had torn from the pad. "Attend to this at once," he ordered.

"Now, Miss Cartwright," he remarked, "I'd like to ask why it was you made this admission about Marie Garnier."

"Because I do not want to see an innocent man go to prison," she returned promptly.

"Oh, I see. And did your sister know it, too?"

"No," she answered quickly.

"Why hadn't you told her?" he demanded.

"Really," said the elder Miss Cartwright with an expression of innocence, "I didn't think it made any difference."

Taylor was obviously annoyed at such a view. "Your behavior is most extraordinary," he commented.

"You see, I know so little about law, and insurance and things like that," she said apologetically. She did not desire to offend him.

"You ought at least to have known that you owed it to the company to give them all the information in your possession," he grumbled.

"I never thought of it in that way," she said meditating.

"There seems a whole lot you young ladies haven't thought of," he said sourly.

Miss Cartwright rose from her seat without haste. "Come, Amy," she commanded. "We can't wait any longer and we are not needed."

As they turned toward the door the telephone bell rang and Taylor stayed them with a gesture. "Just one moment, please, Miss Cartwright."

The girls watching him saw that the news was pleasant for he chuckled as he hung up the receiver. Then he rose from his seat and came to where he stood between them and the door.

"Miss Cartwright," he cried, "when you didn't know what town in Canada your maid was, I felt you were lying. Now I know you were. I just had my assistant telephone to your mother." He pointed an accusing finger at them. "You never had a maid named Garnier, and the last one you had—over a year ago—was called Susan. You put the blame on a woman who doesn't exist, and you did it to shield the real thief." He touched the crouching Amy on the shoulder. "This is the real thief!"

"She isn't, she isn't!" Ethel cried.

But Taylor paid no attention to her. He concentrated his gaze on the younger girl. "You swindled the company," he affirmed.

"No, no," she wailed, "I didn't."

Ethel came to her rescue. "How dare you," she cried to Taylor, "make such an accusation when you have no proof, nor anyone else either?"

"That's all very well," Taylor exclaimed, "but when we get the proof—"

"You can't, because there isn't any," she asserted.

"Of course I see your game," the man said; "you're just trying to protect your sister. That's natural enough, but it will go easier with both of you if you'll tell the truth."

The two girls answered him never a word. Amy was too frightened and Ethel, her tactics unavailing, found her best defense in silence.

"So you won't answer?" Taylor said after a pause. "Well, of course the stuff is pawned some place. That's what they all do. So far, Bronson has only searched the pawn-shops in New York. He didn't give you credit for pawning them outside the city, but I do. Now we'll see where your sister did go." He went to the telephone again. "Hello, Bill," he said when he had secured the number, "Go over to Bronson at the New York and get a description of the jewels reported stolen from a Miss Ethel Cartwright. Have all the pawn-shops searched in Trenton,"—he fastened his harsh look on Amy Cartwright as he called out the names,—"Boston, Washington, Providence, Baltimore, Albany, Philadelphia—"

HE TURNED TO AMY. "YOUNG WOMAN, YOU'RE UNDER ARREST."

As he called out the last city the girl gave a gasp of terror, and triumph instantly lighted up her inquisitor's grim face.

"So you pawned them in Philadelphia?" he cried.

"No, no!" she moaned.

"I did it," Ethel Cartwright exclaimed.

"No, you didn't," Taylor said sharply. "You're only trying to save her. You can't deceive me." He turned to Amy, "Young woman, you're under arrest."

"No, no," the elder sister besought. "Take me. She's only a child; don't spoil her life. I'll do whatever you like; it doesn't matter about me. For God's sake don't do anything to my little sister."

"She's guilty," he reminded her, "and the law says—"

"If somebody pays, what difference does it make to you or the law? Isn't there anything I can do?" she pleaded.

Taylor paced up and down the room for a half minute before answering, while the two watched him in agony. To them he was one who could deliver them over to prison if it were his whim, or spare if he inclined to mercy.

"Surely there is some way out?" Ethel asked again.

"Yes," he said, "there is. You can accept my proposition to enter the secret service of the United States Customs."

"Oh, yes, yes," she cried, "anything!"

Taylor rubbed his hands together with satisfaction and pride in his inimitable craft. "Now you're talking!" he exclaimed. "Then we won't send the little sister to prison."

Amy sobbed relief in her sister's arms.

"Then you won't tell Bronson?" Ethel asked.

"No," he said, "I won't tell Bronson."

Ethel sighed, and felt almost that she would faint.

"Now I'm sorry for you two," Taylor said more genially, "and as long as you do what I tell you to, we'll leave the little matter of the jewels as between your sister and her conscience. I'll let you know when I need you. It may be to-night, it may be not for a month or a year, but when I do want you—"

"I shall be ready," the girl declared.

"Say, Chief," Duncan said looking in at the door,—

"Get out, I'm busy," Taylor shouted.

"I thought you'd like to know the Mauretania was coming up the bay," his satellite returned, slightly aggrieved at this reception.

"She is?" said the other. "Wait a minute then. Now, Miss Cartwright, good afternoon. Remember what is at stake, your future, and your sister's happiness. And don't forget that my silence depends on your not failing me."

Only a man of Taylor's coarse and cruel mould could have looked at her without remorse or compunction. He did not see a beautiful refined woman cheerfully bearing another's cross. He saw only a society girl, who had matched her immature wits against his and lost, was beaten and in the dust. There was a pathetic break in her voice as she answered him.

"I shall not fail you," she said.

Duncan closed the door after them.

"Well?" Taylor demanded eagerly when they were alone. "Did Denby declare the necklace?"

"No, sir," Duncan returned promptly.

"Then I was right," the other commented. "He's trying to smuggle it in. Jim, this is the biggest job we've ever handled."

"Ford and Hammett are at the dock all ready to search him when I give the word."

Duncan was sharing in his chief's triumph, but Taylor's next command was disappointing.

"Don't give the word," he enjoined. "There's to be no search."

"No search?" exclaimed the chagrined Duncan.

"No," Taylor told him. "Just let him slide through with the ordinary examination. Trail Denby and his party to Westbury and be sure none of them slip the necklace to anyone on the way out there, but no fuss and no arrests, remember. Meanwhile, get up a fake warrant for the arrest of Miss Amy Cartwright. It may come in handy."

"Yes, sir," said Duncan obediently.

"And when you've told Ford and Hammett what they are to do, change your clothes and make Gibbs do the same, and meet me at the Pennsylvania Station at six o'clock."

"Where are we going?" Duncan asked. He could see from his chief's manner that something important was in the wind.

"To Long Island," he was told. "We are going to call on Miss Ethel Cartwright."

"Then you can use her to land Denby?" his subordinate cried excitedly.

"Use her?" the deputy-surveyor said with a grim smile. "Say, Jim, she doesn't know it, but she's going to get that necklace for me to-night."

He hurried out of the room, leaving Duncan shaking his head in wonderment. His chief might have qualities that were not endearing, and his manner might at times be rough, but where was there a man who rode through obstacles with the same fine disregard as Daniel Taylor?

CHAPTER SEVEN

MRS. HARRINGTON admitted freely that she had been very far-seeing in asking Denby to travel on the Mauretania with her and Monty. She was one of those modern women who count days damaging to their looks if there comes an hour of boredom in them, and her new acquaintance was always amusing.

One day when they were all three sitting on deck she asked him: "What are you going to do when you get home?"

"Nothing particular," he replied, "except that I want to run down to Washington some time during the month."

"You see," Monty explained, "Steve is a great authority on the tariff. The Secretary of the Treasury does nothing without consulting him. He has to go down and help the cabinet out."

"That's hardly true," Denby said mildly, "but I have friends in Washington nevertheless." It was obvious Monty was not taken in by this. He only regarded his friend as a superb actor who refused to be frightened by the hourly alarms his faithful assistant took to him with fast-beating heart. Young Vaughan told himself a dozen times a day that this excitement, this suspicion of the motives of all strangers, was undermining his health. He had complained of the dull evenness of his existence before meeting Denby in Paris, but he felt such a lament could never again be justified. He found himself unable to sit still for long. He marvelled to see that Denby could sit for hours in a deck-chair talking to Alice without seeming to care whether mysterious strangers were eyeing him or not.

"I asked you," Mrs. Harrington went on, "because, if you've nothing better to do, will you spend a week with us at Westbury? Michael will like you, and if you don't like Michael, there's something seriously wrong with you."

"I'd love to come," he said eagerly. "Thank you very much."

"Hooray," said Monty. "Alice, you're a sweet soul to ask him. Of course he'll like Michael. Who doesn't?"

"Everybody ought to," she said happily. "Do you know, Mr. Denby, I'm one of the only three women in our set who still love their husbands. I wouldn't tell you that except for the reason you'll find out. He's the most generous soul in the world and when I go to him with a bank-book that won't balance, he adds it up and says I've made a mistake and that I'm on the right side. How many husbands would do that?"

"I might," Monty asserted, "because I can't add up long columns, but Michael's a demon at statistics, or used to be."

"He's such an old dear," Mrs. Harrington went on. "His one peculiar talent is the invention of new and strange drinks. I never come back from any long absence but he shows me something violently colored which is built in my honor. And Monty will tell you," she added laughing, "that I have never been seen to shudder while he was looking. Have I, Monty?"

"You're a good sport," said Monty, "and if ever I kill a man, it will be Michael, and my motive will be jealousy."

"Well, you needn't look so unhappy about it," she cried, as a frown passed over his face and he sank back in his chair, all his good-humor gone.

Monty had in that careless phrase, "If ever I kill a man," reminded himself vividly of the dangers that he felt beset him and his friend Steven Denby. He had been trying to forget it and now it was with him to stay. And another and a dreadful thought occurred. Would Denby take those accursed pearls with him to the Harrington mansion on Long Island? It was so disquieting that he rose abruptly and went into a secluded corner of the upper smoking-room and called for a cigar and a pony of brandy.

His attention was presently attracted to a stout comfortable-looking man who was staring at him as though to encourage a bow of recognition. He had noticed the stout and affable gentleman before and always in the same seat, but never before had he sought acquaintance in this manner. There was no doubt in Monty's mind that the man was one of those suave gamblers who reap their richest harvests on the big fast liners. No doubt he knew that Monty was a Vaughan and had occasionally fallen for such professionals and inveigled into a quiet little game. But Monty felt himself of a different sort now.

There was no doubt that the affable gentleman had fully made up his mind as to his plan of action. He rose from his comfortable chair and made his way to the younger man with his hand held out in welcome.

"I thought it was you," he said, and wrung Monty's reluctant hand, "but you are not quite the same as when I saw you last."

"No doubt," Monty said coldly; "I am older and *I* am not the fool I used to be."

"That's good," said the affable gentleman pressing the button that was to summon a steward. "Your father will be glad to hear that."

"Have the kindness to leave my father alone," the younger commanded. Never in his life had Monty found himself able to be so unpleasant. There was, he discovered, a certain joy in it.

"Why, certainly," said the other a trifle startled, "if you wish it. Only as he and I were old friends, I saw no harm in it."

"Old friends?" sneered Monty. "Let me see, you were the same year at Yale, weren't you?"

"Of course," the affable stranger said, and turned to see the advancing steward. "What will you have?" he asked.

"I don't drink with strangers," Monty said rising.

"Strangers!" cried the other with the rising intonation of indignation. "Well, I like that!"

"Then I shall leave you with a pleasant memory," Monty said. "Good day."

"Stop a moment," the stranger asked after a pause in which rage and astonishment chased themselves across his well-nourished countenance. "Who do you think I am, anyway?"

"Your name and number don't interest me," Monty said loftily. He noted that the steward was enjoying it after the quiet inexpressive manner of the English servant. "But I've no doubt at some time or another I lost money to you—your old college friend's money of course—in some quiet game with your confederates."

"Now, what do you think of that!" the red-faced man exclaimed as he watched Monty's retreating figure. But the steward was non-committal. He was not paid to give up his inner thoughts but to bring drinks on a tray.

The stout and affable gentleman was a member of the Stock Exchanges of London and New York and made frequent journeys between these cities. He held the ocean record of having crossed more times and seen the waves less than any stock-broker living. He had passed more hours in a favorite chair in the Mauretania's smoking-room than any man had done since time began. He was raconteur of ability and had been a close friend of the elder Vaughan's years before at Yale. And he burned with fierce indignation when he remembered that he had held the infant Monty years ago and prophesied to a proud mother that he would be her joy and pride. Joy and pride! He snorted and fell away from his true form so far as to seek the deck and suck in fresh air.

There he happened upon Mrs. Harrington talking to Denby. She knew Godfrey Hazen. He had often been to Westbury, and Michael esteemed him for his great knowledge of the proper beverage to take for every emergency that may arise upon an ocean voyage.

"What makes you look so angry?" she exclaimed.

He calmed down when he saw her. "I've just been taken for a professional gambler," he cried.

"I thought all stock-brokers were that," she said smiling.

"I mean a different sort," he explained, "the kind that work the big liners. I just asked him to have a drink when he said he didn't drink with strangers and hinted I had my picture in the rogues' gallery."

"Who was it?" she inquired.

"That ne'er-do-well, Monty Vaughan," he answered.

"Monty?" she said. "Impossible!"

"Is it?" he said grimly. "We'll see. Here comes the young gentleman."

Monty sauntered up without noticing him at first. When he did, he stopped short and was in no whit abashed. "Trying a new game?" he inquired.

"Monty, don't you remember Mr. Hazen?" Alice said reproachfully.

"Have I made an ass of myself?" he asked miserably.

"I wouldn't label any four-footed beast by the name I'd call you," said Mr. Hazen firmly.

"Why didn't you tell me your name?" Monty asked.

"You ought to have remembered me," the implacable Hazen retorted. "Why, I held you in my arms when you were only three months old."

"Then I wish you had dropped me and broken me," Monty exclaimed, "and I should have been spared a lot of worry." Things were piling up to make him more than ever nervous. He had overheard two passengers saying they understood the Mauretania's voyagers were to have a special examination at the Customs on account of diamond smuggling. "I'm sorry, Mr. Hazen," he said more graciously, "but I've things on my mind and you must accept that as the reason."

When he had gone Mr. Hazen was introduced to Denby and prevailed upon to occupy Monty's seat.

"I don't like the look of it," Mr. Hazen said, shaking his head. "At his age he oughtn't to have any worries. I didn't."

"If you can keep a secret," Mrs. Harrington confided, "I think I can tell you exactly what is the matter with Monty and I'm sure you'll make excuses for him, Mr. Hazen."

"Maybe," he returned dubiously, "but you should have heard how he called me down before a steward!"

"Monty's in love," Mrs. Harrington declared, "and after almost two years' absence he is going to meet her again; and the dread of not daring to propose is sapping his brain. You're not the first. He's been out of sorts the whole time and I've had to smooth things over with other people. Come, now," she said coaxingly, "when you were young I'm sure you had some episodes of that sort yourself, now didn't you?"

Mr. Hazen tried not to let her see the proud memories that came surging back through a quarter of a century. "Well," he admitted, "if you put it that way, Mrs. Harrington, I've got to forgive the boy."

"I knew you would," she said, and talked nicely to him for reward.

Then the romance which he had resurrected faded; and the sight of so much salt in the waves—the unaccustomed waves—induced a provoking thirst and he rose and after a conventional lie retired to the smoking-room.

"All the same," Mrs. Harrington remarked to Denby, "I am worried about the boy."

"He'll get over it," said Steven.

"I hope so," she returned. "His nerves are all wrong. I thought he had the absinthe habit at first, but he's really quite temperate, and it's mental, I suspect. It may be Nora; I hope it is. She's a dear girl and Monty's really a big catch."

"Didn't you say you had bought her a present, some valuable piece of jewelry?"

"Which I have sworn to smuggle," she returned brightly, "despite your warning."

"For your sake I wish you wouldn't," he said, "but if your mind's made up, what will my words avail?"

"I'm not stubborn," she cried, "even Michael admits that. I am always open to conviction."

"If you smuggle, you are," he said meaningly. "Really, Mrs. Harrington, you've no idea how strict these examinations are becoming, and this vessel seems specially marked out for extra strict inspections. The popular journals have harped on the fact that the rich, influential women who use this and boats of this class, are exempt, while the woman who saves up for a few weeks' jaunt and brings little inexpensive presents back, is caught."

"Are you sure of that?" she demanded.

"Why, yes," he returned. "It doesn't seem quite fair, does it?" he demanded, looking at her keenly. "It doesn't seem playing the game for the first cabin on the Mauretania to get in free while the second cabin gets caught."

"Have you ever smuggled?" she asked.

"Maybe," he said, "but if I have, it has not been a habit with me as with some rich people I know, who could so easily afford to pay."

"Suppose I do smuggle and get caught, I can pay without any further trouble, can't I?" she queried.

"You're just as likely to be detained," he told her. "To all intents and purposes, it's like being under arrest."

"Oh, Lord!" she cried. "And I shouldn't be able to get back to Michael?"

"Probably not," he said. "You see, Mrs. Harrington, you'd be a splendid tribute to the impartiality of the service. The publicity the Customs people would get from your case would be worth a lot to them. Indirectly, you'd possibly promote hard-working inspectors."

"But I don't want to be a case," she exclaimed, "I'm not anxious to be put in a cell and promote hard-working inspectors. And think of poor Michael all ready with a crimson newly-devised drink pacing the floor while I'm undergoing the third degree! Mr. Denby, I still think the laws are absurd, but I shall declare everything I've got. I wonder if they would let Michael hand me his crimson drink through the bars."

Just then Monty made for them and dropped into his deck-chair.

"I'm going to be an honest woman," she declared, "and smuggle no more. Mr. Denby is the miracle-worker. I shall probably have to borrow money to pay the duty, so be at hand, Monty."

He looked across at Denby and sighed. His friend's serene countenance and absence of nerves was always a source of wonderment to him. Hereafter, he swore, a life in consonance with his country's laws. And if the first few days of the voyage had made him nervous, it was small comfort to think that the really risky part had yet to be gone through. In eliminating Alice Harrington as a fellow smuggler Monty saw extraordinary cunning. "Well," he thought, "if anyone can carry it through it will be old Steve," and rose obediently at Alice's behest and brought back a wireless form on which he indited a message to the absent Michael.

Monty Vaughan had crossed the ocean often, and each time had been cheered to see in the distance the long flat coast-line of his native land. There had always been a sense of pleasurable excitement in the halt at Quarantine and the taking on board the harbor and other officials.

But this time they clambered aboard—the most vindictive set of mortals he had ever laid eyes on—and each one of them seemed to look at Monty as though he recognized a law breaker and a desperado. Incontinently he fled to the smoking-room and ran into the arms of Godfrey Hazen.

"Never mind, my boy," said that genial broker, "you'll soon be out of your misery. Brace up and have a drink. I know how you feel. I've felt like that myself."

"Did you get caught?" Monty gasped.

"No," he said, for he was a bachelor, "but I've had some mighty narrow squeaks and once I thought I was gone."

He watched Monty gulp down his drink with unaccustomed rapidity. "That's right," he said commendingly. "Have another?"

"It would choke me," the younger answered, and fled.

Hazen shook his head pityingly. He had never been as afflicted as the heir to his old friend Vaughan. Poets might understand love and its symptoms but such manifestations were beyond him.

When Steven Denby opened his trunks to a somewhat uninterested inspector and answered his casual questions without hesitation, Monty stood at his side. It cost him something to do so but underneath his apparent timorous nature was a strength and loyalty which would not fail at need.

And when the jaded Customs official made chalk hieroglyphics and stamped the trunks as free from further examination Monty felt a relief such as he had never known. As a poet has happily phrased it, "he chortled in his joy."

"What's the matter?" he demanded of Denby when he observed that his own hilarity was not shared by his companion in danger. "Why not celebrate?"

"We're not off the dock yet," Denby said in a low voice. "They've been too easy for my liking."

"A lot we care," Monty returned, "so long as they're finished with us."

"That's just it," he was warned, "I don't believe they have. It's a bit suspicious to me. Better attend to your own things now, old man."

Monty opened his trunks in a lordly manner. So elaborate was his gesture that an inspector was distrustful and explored every crevice of his baggage with pertinacity. He unearthed with glee a pair of military hair-brushes with backs of sterling silver that Monty had bought in Bond street for Michael Harrington as he passed through London and forgotten in his alarm for bigger things.

"It pays to be honest," said Mrs. Harrington, who had declared her dutiable importations and felt more than ordinarily virtuous. "Monty, you bring suspicion on us all. I'm surprised at you. Just a pair of brushes, too. If you had smuggled in a diamond necklace for Nora there would be some excuse!"

The word necklace made him tremble and he did not trust himself to say a word.

"He's too ashamed for utterance," Denby commented, helping him to repack his trunk.

There were two Harrington motors waiting, both big cars that would carry a lot of baggage. When they were ready it was plain that only two passengers could be carried in one and the third in the second car.

"How shall we manage it?" Mrs. Harrington asked.

"If you don't mind I'll let you two go on," Denby suggested, "and when I've sent off a telegram to my mother, I'll follow."

"I see," she laughed, "you want the stage set for your entrance. Very well. Au revoir."

Monty surprised her by shaking his friend's hand. "Good-by, old man," said Monty sorrowfully. He was not sure that he would ever see Steven again.

CHAPTER EIGHT

MICHAEL HARRINGTON walked up and down the big hall of his Long Island home looking at the clock and his own watch as if to detect them in the act of refusing to register the correct time of day. Although it was probable his wife, Monty and the guest of whose coming a wireless message had apprised him, would not be home for another hour, he was always anxious at such a moment.

He was a man of fifty-eight, exceedingly good-tempered, and very much in love with his wife. When Alice had married a man twenty-four years her senior there had been prophecies that it would not last long. But the two Harringtons had confounded such dismal predictions and lived—to their own vast amusement—to be held up as exemplars of matrimonial felicity in a set where such a state was not too frequent.

His perambulations were interrupted by the entrance of Lambart, a butler with a genius for his service, who bore on a silver tray a siphon of seltzer water, a decanter of Scotch whiskey and a pint bottle of fine champagne.

Lambart had, previously to his importation, valeted the late lamented Marquis of St. Mervyn, an eccentric peer who had broken his noble neck in a steeplechase. Like most English house-servants he was profoundly conservative; and after two positions which he had left because his employers treated him almost as an equal, he had come to the Harringtons and taken a warm but perfectly respectful liking to his millionaire employer. Lambart was a remarkably useful person and it was his proud boast that none had ever beheld him slumbering. Certain it was that a bell summoned him at any hour of the day or night, and he had never grumbled at such calls.

Harrington looked at the refreshment inquiringly. "Did I order this?" he demanded.

"No, sir," Lambart answered, "but my late employer Lord St. Mervyn always said that when he was waiting like you are, sir, it steadied his nerves to have a little refreshment."

"I should have liked the Marquis if I'd known him," Michael Harrington observed when his thirst was quenched. "I think I could have paid him no prettier compliment than to have named a Rocksand colt after him, Lambart. The colt won at Deauville last week, by the way."

"Yes, sir," Lambart returned, "I took the liberty of putting a bit on him; I won, too."

"Good," said his employer, "I'm glad. He ought to have a good season in France. I like France for two things—racing and what they call the *heure de l'aperitif.* When I go to Rome I do as the Romans do, and I have the pleasantest recollections of my afternoons in France."

He noticed that Lambart, bringing over to him a box of cigars, turned his head as though to listen. "I believe, sir," said the butler, "that the car is coming up the drive."

He hurried to the open French window and looked out. "Yes, sir," he cried, "it is one of our cars and Mrs. Harrington is in it."

Michael Harrington rose hastily to his feet. "Great Scott, my wife! The boat must have docked early." He pointed to the whiskey and champagne. "Get rid of these; and not a word, Lambart, not a word."

"Certainly not, sir," Lambart answered; "I couldn't make a mistake of that sort after being with the Marquis of St. Mervyn for seven years."

He took up the tray quickly and carried it off as Nora Rutledge—the girl for whose sake poor Monty had passed hours of alternate misery and hope—came in to tell her host the news.

"Alice is here," she cried, "and Monty Vaughan with her."

Nora was a pretty, clever girl of two and twenty with the up-to-date habit of slangy smartness fully developed and the customary lack of reticence over her love-affairs or those of anyone else in whom she was interested. But for all her pert sayings few girls were more generally liked than she, for the reason that she was genuine and wholesome.

"Fine," Michael said heartily. "Where are they? How is she? Was it a good voyage?"

A moment later his wife had rushed into his arms.

"You dear old thing," she exclaimed affectionately.

"By George! I'm glad to see you," he said, "you've been away for ages."

"You seem to have survived it well enough," she laughed.

"Tell me everything you've done," he insisted.

While she tried to satisfy this comprehensive order, Monty was assuring Nora how delighted he was to see her.

"It's bully to find you here," he said, shaking her hand. "I nearly hugged you."

"Well, why didn't you?" she retorted.

"I've half a mind to," he said, stretching out his arms; but she drew back.

"No. Not now. It's cold. Hugs must be spontaneous."

"Where's Ethel?" Mrs. Harrington called to her.

"Upstairs, changing. You see we didn't think you could get in so early and you weren't expected for another half-hour. She ought to be down in a minute or so."

"Why didn't you come down and meet us, old man?" Monty asked of his host.

"Wife's orders," Harrington responded promptly.

"It's such a nuisance to have people meet one at the pier," Alice explained. "I'm sure Monty was glad you weren't there to witness his humiliation. He was held up for smuggling and narrowly escaped deportation."

"Oh, Monty," Nora cried, "how lovely! Was it something for me? Don't scowl when I ask a perfectly reasonable question."

"It wasn't," Monty said wretchedly. He had in his joy at meeting her forgotten all about smuggling and now the whole thing loomed up again. "I've got half Long Island in my eyes, and if you don't mind, Alice, I'll go and wash up."

"And you won't tell me anything about your crime?" Nora pouted.

"Meet me in the Pagoda in five minutes," he whispered, "and I will. It's mighty nice to see a pretty girl again who can talk American."

"As if men cared what girls say," she observed sagely. "It's the way they look that counts."

When Monty was gone she strolled back to where Alice was sitting.

"Did you have a good trip?" she demanded.

"Bully," Alice answered her. "Steven Denby's most attractive and mysterious."

"Denby!" Harrington repeated. "Why, I'd clean forgotten about Denby. Where is he?"

"The limousine was so full of Monty and me and my hand-baggage that we sent him on in the other car. He had to send some telegrams, so he didn't overtake us till we were this side of Jamaica, where they promptly had a blow-out. He won't be long."

"What Mr. Denby is he?" Nora asked with interest.

"Yes," Michael asked, "do I know him? I don't think I ever heard of him."

"Nor did I," his wife told him. "Perhaps that's what makes him so mysterious."

"Then why on earth have him down here?" her husband asked mildly.

"Because Monty's devoted to him. They were at school together. And also, Michael dear, because I like him and you'll like him. Even if I am married, love has not made me blind to other charming men."

"But, shall I like him?" Nora wanted to know.

"I did the minute I met him," Alice confessed. "He has a sort of 'come hither' in his eyes and the kind of hair I always want to run my hand through. You will, too, Nora."

"But you see I'm not a married woman," Nora retorted, "so I mayn't have your privileges."

Alice laughed. "Don't be absurd. I haven't done it yet—but I may."

"I don't doubt it in the least," said Michael, contentedly caressing her hand.

"He has such an air," Mrs. Harrington explained, "sort of secret and wicked. He might be a murderer or something fascinating like that."

"Splendid fellow for a week-end," her husband commented.

She looked at her watch. "I'd no idea it was so late. I must dress."

"All right," Nora agreed. "Let's see what's become of Ethel."

"Just a minute, Alice," her husband called as she was mounting the broad stairway that led from the hall.

"Run along, Nora," Alice said, "I'll be up in a minute."

"I'll go and wait for Monty," the girl returned. "I think you're going to be lectured." She sauntered out of the French windows toward the Pagoda.

"Well," said Alice smiling, "what is it?"

"I just wanted to tell you how mighty glad I was to see you," he confessed.

"And, Mikey dear," she said simply, "I'm mighty glad to see you."

"Are you really?" he demanded. "You're not missing Paris?"

"Paris be hanged," she retorted; "I'm in love with a man and not with a town."

"It's still me?" Michael asked a little wistfully.

"Always you," she said softly. "One big reason I like to go abroad is because it makes me so glad to get back to you." She sat on the arm of his chair and patted his head affectionately.

"But look here," said Michael with an affectation of reproof, "whenever I want a little trot around the country and suggest leaving, you begin—"

She put her hand over his mouth and stopped him.

"Oh, that's very different. When we do separate I always want to be the one to leave, not to be left."

"It *is* much easier to go than to stay," he agreed, "and I've been pretty lonely these last six weeks."

"But you've had a lot of business to attend to," she reminded him.

"That's finished two weeks ago."

"And then you've had the insidious Lambart and all the Scotch you wanted."

"'Tisn't nearly as much fun to drink when you're away," he insisted. "It always takes the sport out of it not to be stopped."

"Oh, Fibber!" she said, shaking her head.

"Well, most of the sport," he corrected. He held her off at arm's length and regarded her with admiration. "Do you know, I sometimes wonder what ever made you marry me."

"Sometimes I wonder, too," she answered, "but not often! I really think we're the ideal married couple, sentimental when we're alone, and critical when we have guests."

"That's true," he admitted proudly, "and most people hate each other in private and love each other in public." Michael hugged her to emphasize the correctness of their marital deportment.

"You are a dear old thing," she said affectionately.

"Do you know I don't feel a bit married," he returned boyishly, "I just feel in love."

"That's the nicest thing you ever said to me," she said, rising and kissing him. "But I've got to go and find Ethel now."

"You've made me feel fairly dizzy," he asserted, still holding her hand, "I need a drink to sober up."

"Oh, Michael," she cried reprovingly, and drew away from him "I believe you've been trying to get around me just for that!"

"Oh, no, you don't," he said smiling. "Now, do you?"

"No, I don't, Mikey," she admitted. "But be careful, here's Monty and Nora."

"Heavens!" cried Nora, looking in, "still lecturing, you two?"

"You do look rather henpecked," Monty said, addressing his host.

"Yes," Michael sighed, "we've been having a dreadful row, but I'm of a forgiving nature and I'm going to reward her. Monty, touch that button there, I want Lambart."

Alice looked at him in wonderment. "What do you mean?"

"Wait," he said with a chuckle. "Lambart," he commanded, as the butler stood before him, "bring it in." There was respect in his tone. "It ought to be at its best now."

On a silver salver Lambart bore in and presented to his mistress a large liqueur glass filled with a clear liquid of delicate mauve hue.

Alice looked at it a little fearfully. "Oh, Mikey," she said, "is this another new invention?"

"My best," he said proudly.

"Can't I share it?" she pleaded.

"No more than I can my heart," he said firmly. "It is to be named after you."

Heroically she gulped it down.

"Oh, how sweet it is," she exclaimed.

"I know," he admitted. "But as it isn't sugar you needn't mind. I use saccharin which is about a thousand times as sweet. And the beauty of saccharin," he confided to the others, "is that it stays with you. When I first discovered this Crême d'Alicia as I call it, I tasted it for days."

"It's a perfectly divine color," Nora remarked enthusiastically. "I've always dreamed of a dress exactly that shade. How did you do it?"

"Experimenting with the coal tar dyes," he said proudly. "I'm getting rather an expert on coal tar compounds. That color was Perkins' mauve."

"That was more than mauve," Nora insisted. "I've plenty of mauve things."

He raised his hand. "No you don't, Nora! You don't get the result of my years of close study like that. I'll make you each a present of a bottle before you go. We'll have it with coffee every night. Mauve was the foundation upon which I built."

"It's a little rich for me, Mikey dear," his wife said anxiously. "I think it will make a far better winter cordial. I'm going upstairs to see Ethel now."

He watched her disappear and then turned to Nora and Monty with a twinkle in his eye. "I think after my labors I need a little cocktail. In France they call this the *heure de l'aperitif*, as Monty probably knows, and I have a private bar of my own. Don't give me away, children."

Nora looked at her companion with a frown. She had been looking for his coming, and now when he was here, he had nothing to say.

"What's the matter with you?" she demanded suddenly.

"I'm wondering where Steven is," he returned anxiously. "A blow-out oughtn't to keep him all this time."

"But what makes you jump so?" she insisted. "You never used to be like this. Is it St. Vitus's dance?"

He turned to her with an assumption of freedom from care.

"I am a bit nervous, Nora," he admitted. "You see, Steven and I are in a big deal together, and, er, the markets go up and down like the temperature and it keeps me sorts of anxious."

"You don't mean to say you've gone into business?" she said.

"Not exactly," he prevaricated, "and yet I have in a way. It's something secret."

"Well," said Nora, with sound common sense, "if it frightens you so, why go in for it?"

"Well, everything was kind of tepid in Paris," he explained.

"Tepid in Paris?" she cried.

"Why, yes," he told her. "Paris can't always live up to her reputation. I'd been there studying French banking systems so long that I wanted some excitement and joined Steve in his scheme."

"Oh, Monty," she said interested, and sitting on the couch at his side, "if it's really exciting, tell me everything. Are you being pursued?"

He looked at her aggrieved. "Now what do you suggest that for?" he demanded.

"But what is it?" she insisted.

"I can't tell you," he said decidedly. "Steve is one of my oldest friends and I promised him."

"Oh, yes, I've heard all about him," she cried a little impatiently. "You and he went to college together and sang, 'A Stein on the Table,' and went on sprees together and made love to the same girls, and played on the same teams. I know all that college stuff."

"But we didn't go to college together," he said.

"Alice said you did," she returned, "or to school or something together, but don't take that as an excuse to get reminiscent. I hate men's reminiscences; they make me so darned envious. I wish I'd been a man, Monty."

"I don't," said he smiling.

"Don't try to flirt with me," she exclaimed, as he edged a little nearer.

"Why not?" he demanded.

"You don't know how," she said and smiled provokingly.

For a moment Monty forgot pearls and Customs and all unpleasant things.

"Teach me," he entreated.

"It can't be taught," she said. "It's got to be born in you." She cast her eyes down and looked alluringly at him through curling lashes. There was the opportunity for Monty to see whether he had any skill at the ancient game, but a sudden numbing nervousness took hold of him. And while he could have written a prize essay on what he should have done, he had not the courage to make the attempt.

"Well?" she said presently. "Go on."

"I wonder where Steve is?" he said desperately.

"You're hopeless," she cried exasperated. "I don't know where 'Steve' is, and I don't care. I hope he's under the car with gasoline dripping into his eyes."

Poor Monty groaned; for it was equally true that he at this particular moment was anxious to forget everything but the pretty girl at his side.

"Nora," he said nervously, "for the last year there's been something trembling on my lips—"

"Oh, Monty," she cried ecstatically, "don't shave it off, I love it!"

He rose, discomfited, to meet his hostess coming toward him with Miss Ethel Cartwright, a close friend of hers whom he had never before met. He noticed Michael quietly working his unobtrusive way back to the position where Alice had left him, wiping his moustache with satisfaction.

"Monty," said Mrs. Harrington, "I don't think you've ever met my very best friend, Miss Cartwright."

"How do you do," the girl said smiling.

"Be kind to him, Ethel," Michael remarked genially. "He's a nice boy and the idol of the Paris Bourse."

"And an awful flirt," Nora chimed in. "If I had had a heart he would have broken it long ago."

"Do you know," Alice said, "it has never occurred to me to think of Monty as a flirt. Are you a flirt, Monty?"

"No," he said indignantly.

"You needn't be so emphatic when I ask you," she said reprovingly. She sighed. "I suppose it's one of the penalties of age. I've known him a disgracefully long time, Ethel, before the Palisades were grown-up."

"I'm sorry I didn't get down to meet you, Alice," Miss Cartwright said, "I did mean to, but business detained me."

"Business in August!" Nora commented.

"I'm glad you didn't," her hostess observed. "We were disgraced by having in our merry party a smuggler who was caught with the goods and narrowly escaped Sing Sing."

"There you go again," Monty grumbled. "I hate the very sound of the word."

"I say, Ethel," Michael observed, watching her closely, "you do look a bit pale. Business in weather like this doesn't suit you. No bad news, I hope?"

He knew that the division of the late Vernon Cartwright's fortune was very disappointing and might narrow the girls' income considerably.

"It turned out all right, thank you," the girl answered nervously.

"How's Amy?" Mr. Harrington asked. He was fond of the Cartwrights and had known them from childhood. "Why isn't she here?"

"It isn't to be a big party, Michael," his wife reminded him. "Men are so scarce in August I didn't ask Amy. She's all right, I hope, Ethel?"

"Yes, thanks," Miss Cartwright answered.

"I wonder where Steve is?" Monty said for the fifth time. "He ought to have that tire fixed by now."

"I hope he hasn't smashed up," said Alice.

"So do I," Michael retorted. "It was a mighty good car—almost new—and I left a silver pocket-flask in it, I remember."

"Is someone else coming?" Ethel Cartwright asked.

"A perfectly charming man, a Steven Denby."

"Steven Denby?" Miss Cartwright cried, her face lighting up. "Really?"

"Do you know him then?" Mrs. Harrington asked.

"Indeed I do," she answered.

"What, you know Steve?" Monty asked in surprise.

"Tell us about him," Nora besought her.

"Yes, who is he?" Michael wanted to know. "Alice has been trying to rouse me to the depths of my jealous nature about him!"

"Isn't he fascinating?" Alice observed.

"I can only tell you all," Ethel Cartwright declared, "that I know him. I met him in Paris a year ago."

"Didn't you like him?" Alice inquired.

"I did, very much," the girl said frankly.

Nora spoke in a disappointed manner. "Well, he's evidently yours for this week-end."

"I daresay he won't even remember me," the other girl returned.

"Oh, I bet he will," said Nora, who was able to give Ethel credit for her charm and beauty. "I shall just have to stick around with Monty—a wild tempestuous flirt like Monty!"

"Oh, I don't mind," Monty said with an air of condescension, "not particularly."

"It's time to dress, good people," Michael reminded them.

"Come on, Nora," Alice said rising. "Come, Monty. Ethel, you'll have to amuse yourself, as Michael isn't to be depended on."

"You wrong me, my dear," Michael retorted. "I'm going for my one solitary cocktail and then I'll be back."

"And only one, remember," Alice warned him.

"You know me, my dear," he said, "when I say one."

"You sometimes mean only one at a time," she laughed. "You are still the same consistent old Michael. And by the way, if Mr. Denby does happen to turn up, tell him we'll be down soon."

"I'll send him in to Ethel if he comes."

"Yes, please do," the girl said brightly.

When she was left alone in the big hall, the coolest apartment in the big house during the afternoon, Ethel Cartwright went to the French windows and looked out over the smooth lawns to the trees at the back of them. A long drive wound its way to the highroad, up which she could see speeding a big motor. The porte-cochère was at the other side of the house and she retraced her steps to the hall she had left with the hope of meeting the man she had liked so much a year ago in Paris.

A minute later he was ushered in, but did not at first see her. Then, as he looked about the big apartment, he caught sight of the girl, and stood for a moment staring as though he could hardly venture to believe it was she.

"Miss Cartwright," he cried enthusiastically, "is it really you?"

She took his outstretched hands graciously. "How do you do, Mr. Denby," she said.

"Mr. Harrington told me to expect a surprise," he cried, "but I was certainly not prepared for such a pleasant one as this. How are you?"

"Splendid," she answered. "And you?"

"Very, very grateful to be here."

"I wondered if you'd remember me," she said; "it's a long time ago since we were in Paris."

"It was only the day before yesterday," he asserted.

"And what are you doing here?" she asked.

"Oh, I thought I'd run over and see if New York was finished yet."

"Are you still doing—nothing?" she demanded, a tinge of disappointment in her voice.

He looked at her with a smile. "Still—nothing," he answered.

"Ah," she sighed, "I had such hopes of you, a year ago in Paris."

"And I of you," he said, boldly looking into her eyes.

Her manner was more distant now. "I'm afraid I don't admire idlers very much. Why don't you do something? You've ability enough, Mr. Denby."

"It's so difficult to get a thrill out of business," he complained.

"And you must have thrills?" she asked.

"Yes," he answered, "it's such a dull old world nowadays."

"Then why," she exclaimed jestingly, "why don't you take to crime?"

"I have thought of it," he laughed, "but the stake's too high—a thrill against prison."

"So you want only little thrills then, Mr. Denby?"

"No," he told her, "I'd like big ones better. Life or even death—but not prison. And what have you done since I saw you last? You are still doing nothing, too?"

"Nothing," she said, smiling.

"And you're still Miss Cartwright?"

"*Only* Miss Cartwright," she corrected.

"Good," he said, looking at her steadily. "By George, it doesn't seem a year since that week in Paris. What made you disappear just as we were having such bully times?"

"I had to come back to America suddenly. I had only an hour to catch the boat. I explained all that in my note though. Didn't you even take the trouble to read it?"

He looked at her amazed. "I never even received it." There was a touch of relief in his voice. "So you sent me a note! Do you know, I thought you'd dropped me, and I tell you I hit with an awful crash."

"I sent it by a porter and even gave him a franc," she smiled. "I ought to have given him five."

"I'd willingly have given him fifty," Denby said earnestly. "It wasn't nice to think that I'd been dropped like that."

"And I thought you'd dropped me," she said.

"I should say not," he exclaimed. "I was over here six months ago and I did try to see you, but you were at Palm Beach. I can't tell you how often I've sent you telepathic messages," he added whimsically. "Ever get any of 'em?"

"Some of them, I think," she said smiling. "And now to think we've met here on Long Island. It's a far cry to Paris."

"For me it's people who make places—the places themselves don't matter—you and I are here," he said gently.

The girl sighed a little. "Still, Paris is Paris," she insisted.

"Rather!" he answered, sighing too. "Do you remember that afternoon in front of the Café de la Paix? We had *vin gris* and watched the Frenchman with the funny dog, and the boys calling *La Presse*, and the woman who made you buy some 'North Wind' for me, and the people crowding around the newspaper kiosks."

In the adjoining room Nora was strumming the piano, and was now playing "*Un Peu d'Amour.*" She had looked in the hall and finding the stranger so wholly absorbed in Ethel Cartwright, had retired to solitude.

"And do you remember the hole in the table-cloth?" Ethel demanded.

"And wasn't it a dirty table-cloth?" he reminded her. "And afterwards we had tea in the Bois at the Cascade and the Hungarian Band played '*Un Peu d'Amour.*'" He looked at the girl smiling. "How did you arrange to have that played just at the right moment?"

They listened in silence for a moment to the dainty melody, and then she hummed a few bars of it. Her thoughts were evidently far away from Long Island.

"And don't you remember that poor skinny horse in our fiacre?" she asked him. "He was so tired he fell down, and we walked home in pity."

"Ah, you were tender-hearted," he sighed.

"And we had dinner at Vian's afterwards," she reminded him, and then, after a pause: "Wasn't the soup awful?"

"Ah, but the string-beans were an event," he asserted. "And that evening, I remember, there was a moon over the Bois, and we sat under the trees. Have you forgotten that?"

"I don't think that would be very easy," she said softly.

"And we went through the Louvre the next day," he said eagerly, "the whole Louvre in an hour, and the loveliest picture I saw there was—*you.*"

Denby glanced up with a frown as Lambart's gentle footfall was heard, and rose to his feet a trifle embarrassed by this intrusion. Lambart came to a respectful pause at Miss Cartwright's side.

"Pardon me," he said, "but there is a gentleman to see you." She took a card that was on the tray he held before her.

"To see me?" she cried, startled, gazing at the card. Denby, watching her closely, saw her grow, as he thought, pale. "Ask him to come in. Mr. Denby," she said, "will you forgive me?"

"Surely," he assented, walking toward the great stairway. "I have to dress, anyway."

"Your room is at the head of the stairs," Lambart reminded him. "All your luggage is taken in, sir."

Denby looked down at her. "Till dinner?" he asked.

"Till dinner," she said, and watched him pass out of sight. She was a girl whose poise of manner prevented the betrayal of vivid emotion in any but a certain subdued fashion. But it was plain she was laboring now under an agitation that amounted almost to deadly fear.

A few seconds later Daniel Taylor strode in with firm assured tread and looked at the luxurious surroundings with approval.

"Good evening, Miss Cartwright," he exclaimed genially. "Good evening."

"My sister," she returned, trembling, "nothing's happened to her? She's all right?"

"Sure, sure," he returned reassuringly, "I haven't bothered her; the little lady's all right, don't you worry."

"Then what do you want here?" she cried alarmed. No matter what his manner this man had menace in every look and gesture. She had never been brought into contact with one who gave in so marked a degree the impression of ruthless strength.

"I thought I'd drop in with reference to our little chat this afternoon," he remarked easily. "Nice place they've got here."

"But I don't understand why you have come," she persisted.

"You haven't forgotten our little conversation, I hope?"

"Of course not," she said.

"Well," he continued, "you said when I needed you, you'd be ready." He looked about him cautiously as though fearing interruption. "I said it might be a year, or it might be a month, or it might be to-night. Well, it's to-night, Miss Cartwright. I need you right now."

"Now?" she said puzzled. "Still, I don't understand."

He lowered his voice. "A man has smuggled a two hundred thousand dollar necklace through the Customs to-day. For various reasons which you wouldn't understand, we allowed him to slip through, thinking he'd fooled us. Now that he believes himself safe, it ought to be easy to get that necklace. We've got to get it; and we're going to get it, through one of our agents." He pointed a forefinger at her. "We're going to get it through you."

"But I shouldn't know how to act," she protested, "or what to do."

Taylor smiled. "You're too modest, Miss Cartwright. I've seen some of your work in my own office, and I think you'll be successful."

"But don't you see I'm staying here over Sunday?" she explained. "I can't very well make an excuse and leave now."

"You don't have to leave," he told her.

"What do you mean, then?" she demanded.

"That the man who smuggled the necklace is staying here, too. His name is Steven Denby."

"Steven Denby!" the girl cried, shrinking away from him. "Oh, no, you must be mad—he isn't a smuggler."

"Why isn't he?" Taylor snapped.

"I know him," she explained.

"You do?" he cried. "Where did you meet him?"

"In Paris," she replied.

"How long have you known him?"

"Just about a year," she answered.

"What do you know about him?" Taylor asked quickly. It was evident that her news seemed very important to him. "What's his business? How does he make his living? Do you know his people?"

"I don't think he does anything," she said hesitatingly.

"Nothing, eh?" Taylor laughed disagreeably. "I suppose you think that's clear proof he couldn't be a smuggler?"

"I'm sure you are wrong," she said with spirit; "he's my friend."

"Your friend!" Taylor returned. His manner from that of the bluff cross-examiner changed to one that had something confidential and friendly in it. "Why, that ought to make it easier."

"Easier?" she repeated. "What do you mean by that?"

"Well, you can get into his confidence. See?"

"But you're wrong," she said indignantly. "I'm sure he is absolutely innocent."

"Then you'll be glad of a chance to prove we're wrong and you're right."

"But I couldn't spy on a friend," she declared.

"If your friend is innocent it won't do him any harm," Taylor observed, "and he'd never know. But if he's guilty he deserves punishment, and you've no right to try and protect him. Any person would only be doing right in helping to detect a criminal; but you,"—he paused significantly,—"it's just as much your duty as it is mine." He showed her his gold badge of authority for a brief moment, and although it terrified her there was too much loyalty in her nature to betray a friend or even to spy upon one.

"No, no! I can't do it," she said.

"So you're going back on your agreement," he sneered. "Two can play that game. Suppose I go back on mine, too?"

"You wouldn't do that," she cried horrified at his threat.

"Why not?" he returned. "It's give and take in this world."

"But I couldn't be so contemptible."

Taylor shrugged his shoulders. "If I were you I'd think it over," he recommended.

"But supposing you're wrong," she said earnestly. "Suppose he has no necklace?"

"Don't let that disturb you," he retorted. "Our information is positive. We got a telegram late this afternoon from a pal of his who squealed, giving us a tip about it. Now what do you say?"

"I can't," she said, "I can't."

He came closer, and said in a low harsh voice: "Remember, it's Steven Denby or your sister. There's no other way out. Which are you going to choose?"

He watched her pale face eagerly. "Well," he cried, "which is it to be?"

"I have no choice," she answered dully. "What do you want me to do?"

"Good," Taylor cried approvingly. "That's the way to talk! Denby has that necklace concealed in a brown leather tobacco-pouch which he always carries in his pocket. You must get me that pouch."

"How can I?" she asked despairingly.

"I'll leave that to you," he answered.

"But couldn't you do it?" she pleaded. "Or one of your men? Why ask me?"

"It may be a bluff, some clever scheme to throw me off the track and I'm not going to risk a mix-up with the Harringtons or tip my hand till I'm absolutely sure. It don't pay me to make big mistakes. You say Denby's your friend, well, then, it'll be easy to find out. If you discover that the necklace is in the tobacco-pouch, get him to go for a walk in the garden; say you want to look at the moon, say anything, so long as you get him into the garden where we'll be on the lookout and grab him."

"But he might go out there alone," she suggested.

"If he does," Taylor assured her, "we won't touch him, but if he comes out there with you, we'll *know*."

"But if I can't get him into the garden?" she urged. "Something may happen to prevent me!"

"If you're sure he has it on him," Taylor instructed her, "or if you make out where it is concealed, pull down one of these window-shades. My men and I can see these from the garden. When we get your signal we'll come in and arrest him. Sure you understand?"

"I'm to pull down the window-shade," she repeated.

"That's it, but be careful, mind. Don't bring him out in the garden, and don't signal unless you are absolutely certain."

"Yes, yes," she said.

"And under no circumstances," he commanded, "must you mention my name."

"But," she argued, "suppose—"

"There's no 'buts' and no 'supposes' in it," he said sharply. "It's most important to the United States Government and to me, that my identity is in no way disclosed."

"It may be necessary," she persisted.

"It *cannot* be necessary," he said with an air of finality. "If it comes to a show-down and you tell Denby I'm after him, I'll not only swear I never saw you, but I'll put your sister in prison. Now, good night, Miss Cartwright, and remember you've got something at stake, too, so don't forget—Denby to-night."

He went silently through the French windows and disappeared, leaving her to face for the second time in a day an outlook that seemed hopeless.

But she was not the only one in the great Harrington mansion to feel that little zest was left in life. Monty was obsessed with the idea that his friend's long delay was due to his having been held up. The automobile lends itself admirably to highway robbery, and it would be easy enough for armed robbers to overpower Denby and the chauffeur.

Directly he heard Denby's voice talking to Lambart as he was shown into his room, Monty burst in and wrung his hands again and again.

"Why, Monty," his friend said, "you overpower me."

"I thought you'd been held up and robbed," the younger man cried.

"Neither one nor the other," Denby said cheerfully, "I was merely the victim of two blow-outs. But," he added, looking keenly at his confederate, "if I had been held up the pearls wouldn't have been taken. I didn't happen to have them with me."

"Thank God!" Monty cried fervently. "I wondered if that telegraphing to people was just a ruse or not. Hooray, I feel I can eat and drink and be merrier than I've been for a month. I never want to hear about them again."

"I'm sorry, old man," Denby said smiling, "but I shall have to ask you for them."

"Me?" Monty stammered. "Don't joke, Steve."

"But you very kindly brought them over for me," Denby returned mildly. "They're in the right-hand shoe of a pair of buckskin tennis shoes. I put them there when I helped you to repack your trunk. Do you mind bringing them before I've finished dressing?"

Monty looked at him reproachfully. "Sometimes I think I ought to have gone into the ministry. I'm getting a perfect horror of crime."

"You're not a criminal," Denby said. "You helped me out on the voyage, but here you are free to do as you like."

Monty set his jaw firmly. "I'm in it with you, Steve, till you've got the damned things where you want 'em, and you can't prevent me, either."

When he brought the precious necklace back Denby calmly placed the pouch in his pocket. "Thanks, old man," he said casually. "Now the fun begins."

"Fun!" Monty snorted. "Do you remember the classic remark of the frog who was pelted by small mischievous boys? 'This may be the hell of a joke to you,' said the frog, 'but it's death to me.'"

"I've always been sorry for that frog," Denby commented.

"But, man alive, you are the frog," Monty cried.

"Oh, no," Denby returned, making a tie that had no likeness to a vast butterfly.

"Your frog hadn't a ghost of a chance, and he knew it, while with me it's an even chance. One oughtn't to ask any more than that in these hard times."

He sauntered down the stairs cool and debonair to find Ethel Cartwright still looking listlessly across the green lawns.

"Those gentle chimes," he said, as the dinner-gong pealed out, "call the faithful to dinner. I wish it were in Paris, don't you?"

She pulled herself together and tried to smile as she had done before Taylor had dashed all her joy to the ground.

"Aren't you hungering for string-beans?" he asked, "and the hole in the table-cloth, and the gay old moon? But after all, what do they matter now? You're here, and I'm hungry." He offered her his arm. "Aren't you hungry, too?"

CHAPTER NINE

VERY much to Denby's disappointment he found that he was not to take Ethel Cartwright in to dinner. Nora Rutledge fell to his lot, and although she was witty and sparkling, she shared none of those happy Parisian memories as did the girl his host had taken in.

Plainly Nora was piqued. "I thought from what Monty told me you were really interesting," she said.

"One must never believe anything Monty says," he observed. "It's only his air of innocence that makes people think him honest. His flirtations on board ship were nothing short of scandalous and yet look at him now."

And poor Monty, although to him had fallen the honor of taking in his hostess, was paying no sort of attention to her sallies.

Nora glanced at him and then looked up at Denby. "I'm really awfully fond of Monty, and I'm worried—if you'll believe it—because he seems upset. Monty," she called, "what's the matter with you, and what are you thinking about?"

"Frogs," he said promptly.

"We'll have some to-morrow," Michael observed amiably. "They induce in me a most remarkable thirst, so I keep off them on that account."

"He's thinking," Denby reminded her, "of the old song, 'A frog he would a-wooing go!' I've heard of you often enough, Miss Rutledge, from Monty."

"Well, I wish you'd started being confidential with the *hors d'œuvres*," she said, "instead of waiting until dessert. If you had, by this time you'd probably have been really amusing."

She rose at Mrs. Harrington's signal and followed her from the room.

"What I can't see," observed she, "is why we didn't stay and have our cigarettes with the men."

"I always leave them together," Alice Harrington said with a laugh, "because that's the way to get the newest naughty stories. Michael always tells 'em to me later."

"Alice!" cried Nora with mock reproof.

"Oh, I like 'em," Alice declared, "when they're really funny, and so does everybody else. Besides, nowadays it's improper to be proper. Cigarette, Ethel?"

Miss Cartwright shook her head. "You know I don't smoke," she returned.

Nora lighted a cigarette unskilfully. "That's so old-fashioned," she said, in her most sophisticated manner, "and I'd rather die than be that." She coughed as she drew in a fragrant breath of Egyptian tobacco. "I do wish, though, that I really enjoyed smoking."

"What do you think of our new friend, Mr. Denby?" Alice asked of her.

"I like him in spite of the fact that he hardly noticed me. He couldn't take his eyes off Ethel."

"I saw that myself," Mrs. Harrington returned. "You know, Ethel, I meant him to take you in to dinner, but Nora insisted that she sit next to him. She's such a man-hunter!"

"You bet I am," the wise Nora admitted—"that's the only way you can get 'em."

Mrs. Harrington turned to Ethel Cartwright. "Didn't you and Mr. Denby have a tiny row? You hardly spoke to him through dinner."

"Didn't I?" the girl answered. "I've a bit of a headache."

"I'll bet they had a lovers' quarrel before dinner," Nora hazarded.

Alice Harrington arched her eyebrows in surprise. "A lovers' quarrel!"

"Certainly," Nora insisted. "I'm sure Ethel is in love with him."

"How perfectly ridiculous," Ethel said, with a trace of embarrassment in her manner. "Don't be so silly, Nora. I met him for a week in Paris, that's all, and I found him interesting. He had big talk as well as small, but as for love—please don't be idiotic!"

"Methinks the lady doth protest too much," laughed her hostess.

"I don't blame you, Ethel," Nora admitted frankly. "If he'd give me a chance I'd fall for him in a minute, but attractive young men never bother about me. The best I can draw is—Monty! I'm beginning to dislike the whole sex."

"Theoretically you are quite right, my dear," said the maturer Alice; "men are awful things—God bless 'em—but practically, well, some day you'll explode like a bottle of champagne and bubble all over some man."

"Speaking of champagne," Nora said after a disbelieving gesture at the prophecy, "I wish I had another of Michael's purple drinks. He's a genius."

"Do tell him that," the fond wife urged. "The very surest way to Michael's heart is through his buffet. I knew he'd taken to mixing cocktails in a graduated chemist's glass, but this excursion into the chemistry of drinks is rather alarming. He would have been a most conscientious bartender."

"Does he really drink much?" Nora demanded.

"Not when I'm at home," Alice declared. "Nothing after one. If he goes to bed then he's all right; if he doesn't, he sits up till five going the pace that fills. I wouldn't mind if it made him amusing, but it makes him merely sleepy. But he doesn't drink nearly as much as most of the men he knows. What makes you think he does, is that he makes such a ceremony out of drinking. I don't think he enjoys drinking alone. Nora," she added, "do sit down; you make me dizzy."

"I can't," Nora told her. "I always stand up for twenty minutes after each meal. It keeps you thin."

"Does it?" Mrs. Harrington asked eagerly, rising from her comfortable chair. "Does it really? Still, I lost nine pounds abroad!"

"Goodness!" Nora cried enviously. "How?"

"Buttermilk!" Alice cried triumphantly.

"And I walked four miles this morning in a rubber suit and three sweaters, *and* gained half a pound," Nora declared disconsolately.

"I do wish hips would come in again," Alice Harrington sighed. "Ah, here come the men," she said more brightly, as the three entered.

Michael was still bearing, with what modesty he could, the encomiums on a purple punch he had brewed after exhaustive laboratory experiments.

"It's delicious," Denby declared.

Michael sighed. "I used to think so until my wife stopped my drinking."

Even Monty seemed cheered by it. "Fine stuff," he asserted. "I can feel it warming up all the little nooks and crannies."

"Purple but pleasing," Denby said, with the air of an epigrammatist.

"Did they tell you any purple stories?" Michael's wife demanded.

"We don't know any new stories," Denby told her; "we've been in England."

"Do sit down, all of you," Alice commanded. "We've all been standing up to get thin."

"If they're going to discuss getting thin and dietetics," Michael said, "let's get out."

"Woman's favorite topic," Monty remarked profoundly.

"But you mustn't sit down, Alice," Nora warned, as her hostess seemed about to sink into her chair. "It isn't twenty minutes!"

"Well, I think it is twenty minutes," she returned smiling, "and if it isn't I don't care a continental."

"Women are so self-denying," Michael Harrington observed with gentle satire.

"And sometimes it pays," his wife said. "Do you know, Nora, there was a girl on the boat who lost twelve pounds."

"Twelve pounds," Michael exclaimed, and then by a rapid-fire bit of mental arithmetic added: "Why, that's sixty dollars. How women do gamble nowadays!"

"Pounds of flesh, Michael, pounds of flesh. She was on a diet. She didn't eat for three days."

"That's not a bad idea," Nora said approvingly. "Sometime when I'm not hungry I'll try it."

Ethel Cartwright had refrained from joining in the conversation for the reason she had no part just now in their lighter moods. Their talk of weight losing had been well enough, but Michael's misinterpretation of the twelve pounds brought back to her the cause of Amy's misfortune and plunged her deeper into misery.

She walked toward the window and looked over the grass to the deep gloom of the cedar trees opposite. And it seemed to her that there were moving shadows that might be Taylor and his men ready to pounce upon a man to whom a year ago she had been deeply drawn. There was a charm about Denby when he set himself to please a woman to which she, although no blushing ingénue, was keenly sensible.

"Seeing ghosts?" said a voice at her elbow, and she turned, startled, to see his smiling face looking down at her.

She assumed a lighter air. "No," she told him brightly. "Ghosts belong to the past. I was seeing spirits of the future."

"Can't we see them together?" he suggested. "I shall never tire of Parisian ghosts if you are there to keep me from being too scared. Let's go out and see if the moon looks good-tempered. The others are talking about smuggling and light and airy nothings like that. Shall we?"

"No, no!" she said, with a tremor in her voice that did not escape him. "Not yet; later, perhaps."

She could, in fact, hardly compose her face. Here he was suggesting that she take him into a trap to be prepared later by her treachery. But she had what seemed to her a duty to perform, and no sentiment must stand in the way of her sister's salvation. And there was always the hope that he was innocent. At any other time than this she would have wagered he was without blame; but this was a day on which misfortunes were visiting her, and she was filled with dread as to its outcome.

She moved over to Mrs. Harrington's side, gracefully and slowly, free so far as the ordinary observer could see from any care.

"So you are talking of smuggling," she said. "Alice, did you really bring in anything without paying duty on it?"

"Not a thing," Alice returned promptly. "I declared every solitary stitch."

"I'd like to believe you," her husband remarked, "but knowing you as I do—"

"I paid seven hundred dollars' duty," his spouse declared.

"Disgusting!" Nora exclaimed. "Think of what you could have bought for that!"

"Please tell me," Michael inquired anxiously, "what mental revolution converted you from the idea that smuggling was a legitimate and noble sport?"

"I still don't think it's wrong," Alice declared honestly. "Some of you men seem to, but I'd swindle the government any day."

"Then, for Heaven's sake," Nora wanted to know, "why waste all that good money?"

Alice waved a jewelled white hand toward Steven Denby.

"Behold my reformer!"

Ethel Cartwright looked at him quickly. Her distrust of motives was the result of her conversation with Daniel Taylor, who believed in no man's good faith.

"Mr. Denby?" she asked, almost suspiciously.

"What has Mr. Denby to do with it?" Nora cried, equally surprised that it was his influence which had stayed the wilful Alice.

"He frightened me," Alice averred.

"I want to have a good look at the man who can do that," Michael cried.

"I'm afraid Mrs. Harrington is exaggerating," Denby explained patiently; "I merely pointed out that things had come to a pass when it might be very awkward to fool with the Customs."

"They didn't give us the least bit of trouble at the dock," she answered. "I wish I'd brought in a trunk full of dutiable things. They hardly looked at my belongings."

"That sometimes means," Denby explained, "that there will be the greatest possible trouble afterwards."

"I don't see that," Nora asserted. "How can it be?"

"Well," he returned, "according to some articles in McClure's a few months ago by Burns, very often a dishonest official will let a prominent woman like Mrs. Harrington slip through the lines without the least difficulty—even if she is smuggling—so that afterwards he can come to her home and threaten exposure and a heavy fine. Usually the woman or her husband will pay any amount to hush things up. I was thinking of that when I advised Mrs. Harrington to declare everything she had."

"But you said a whole lot more than that," Mrs. Harrington reminded him. "When our baggage was being examined at Dover, you spoke about that man of mystery who is known as R. J. It was cumulative, Mr. Denby, and on the whole you did it rather well. My bank-book is a living witness to your eloquence."

Ethel asked rather eagerly, "But this R. J., Mr. Denby, what is he?"

"I've heard of him," Michael answered. "Some man at the club told me about him, but I very soon sized that matter up. If you want to know my opinion, Ethel, R. J. is the bogey man of the Customs. If they suspect an inspector he receives a postal signed R. J., and telling him to watch out. It's a great scheme, which I recommend to the heads of big business corporations. I don't believe in R. J."

Ethel looked up at Denby brightly. "But you really believe in him, don't you?"

"I only know," he told her, "that R. J. has many enemies because he has made many discoveries. Unquestionably he does exist for all Mr. Harrington's unbelief. He's supposed to be one of these impossible secret service agents, travelling incognito all over the globe. He is known only by his initials. Some people call him the storm-petrol, always in the wake of trouble. Where there is intrigue among nations, diplomatic tangles, if the Japs steal a fortification plan, or a German cross-country aeroplane is sent to drop a bomb on the Singer Building, R.J. is supposed to be there to catch it."

"What an awfully unpleasant position," Nora shuddered.

"Think of a man deliberately choosing a job like that!" Monty commented.

"So," Denby continued, "when a friend of mine in Paris told me that R.J. had been requested by the government to investigate Customs frauds, I knew there would be more danger in the smuggling game than ever. I warned Mrs. Harrington because I did not want to see her humiliated by exposure."

"That's mighty good of you, Denby," Michael said appreciatively; "but all the same I don't see how—supposing she had slipped in without any fuss some stuff she had bought in Paris or London and ought to have declared—I don't see how if they didn't know it, they could blackmail her."

"That's the simplest part of it," Denby assured him. "The clerk in the kind of store your wife would patronize is most often a government spy, unofficially, and directly after he has assured the purchaser that it is so simple to smuggle, and one can hide things so easily, he has cabled the United States Customs what you bought and how much it cost."

"They do that?" said Michael indignantly. "I never did trust Frenchmen, the sneaks. I've no doubt that the *heure de l'aperitif* was introduced by an American."

Miss Cartwright had been watching Denby closely. There was forced upon her the unhappy conviction that this explanation of the difficulties of smuggling was in a sense his way of boasting of a difficulty he had overcome. And she alone of all who were listening had the key to this. It was imperative—for the dread of Taylor and his threats had eaten into her soul—to gain more explicit information. Her manner was almost coquettish as she asked him:

"Tell me truly, Mr. Denby, didn't you smuggle something, just one tiny little scarf-pin, for example?"

"Nothing," he returned. "What makes you think I did?"

"It seemed to me," she said boldly, "that your fear that Mrs. Harrington might be caught was due to the fear suspicion might fall on you."

Denby looked at her curiously. He had never seen Ethel Cartwright in this mood. He wondered at what she was driving.

"It does sound plausible," he admitted.

"Then 'fess up," Michael urged. "Come on, Denby, what did you bring in?"

"Myself and Monty," Denby returned, "and he isn't dutiable. All the smuggling that our party did was performed by Monty out of regard for you."

"I still remain unconvinced," Ethel Cartwright declared obstinately. "I think it was two thoughts for yourself and one for Alice."

"Now, Denby," Michael cried jocularly, "you're among friends. Where have you hidden the swag?"

"Do tell us," Nora entreated. "It'd be so nice if you were a criminal and had your picture in the rogues' gallery. The only criminals I know are those who just run over people in their motors, and that gets so commonplace. Do tell us how you started on a life of crime."

"Nora!" Monty cried reprovingly. Things were increasing his nervousness to a horrible extent. Why wouldn't they leave smuggling alone?

"I'm not interested in your endeavors," Nora said superciliously. "You're only a sort of petty larceny smuggler with your silver hair-brushes. Mr. Denby does things on a bigger scale. You're safe with us, Mr. Denby," she reminded him.

"I know," he answered, "so safe that if I had any dark secrets to reveal I'd proclaim them with a loud voice."

"That's always the way," Nora complained. "Every time I meet a man who seems exciting he turns out to be just a nice man—I hate nice men." She crossed over to the agitated Monty.

"Mr. Denby is a great disappointment to me, too," Ethel Cartwright confessed. "Couldn't you invent a new way to smuggle?"

"It wasn't for lack of inventive powers," he assured her, "it was just respect for the law."

"I didn't know we had any left in America," Michael observed, and then added, "but then you've lived a lot abroad, Denby."

"Mr. Denby must be rewarded with a cigarette," Ethel declared, bringing the silver box from the mantel and offering him one. "A cigarette, Mr. Denby?"

"Thanks, no," he answered, "I prefer to roll my own if you don't mind."

It seemed that the operation of rolling a cigarette was amazingly interesting to the girl. Her eager eyes fastened themselves intently on a worn pigskin pouch he carried.

"Can't you do it with one hand?" she asked disappointedly; "just like cowboys do in plays?"

"It seems I'm doomed to disappoint you," he smiled. "I find two hands barely sufficient."

"Sometime you must roll me one," she said. "Will you?"

"With pleasure," he returned, lighting his own.

"But you don't smoke," Alice objected.

"Ah, but I've been tempted," she confessed archly.

"The only thing that makes my life worth living is yielding to temptation," Nora observed.

"That's not a bad idea," Michael said rising. "I'm tempted to take a small drink. Who'll yield with me and split a pint of Brut Imperial?"

"That's your last drink to-night," his wife warned him.

"I'm not likely to forget it," he said ruefully. "My wife," he told the company, "thinks I'm a restaurant, and closes me up at one sharp."

"Let's have some bridge," Mrs. Harrington suggested. "Ethel, what do you say?"

"I've given it up," she answered.

"Why, you used to love it," Nora asserted, surprised.

"I've come to think all playing for money is horrible," Ethel returned, thinking to what trouble Amy's gambling had brought her.

"Me too," Michael chimed in. "Unless stocks go up, or the Democratic party goes down, I'll be broke soon. How about a game of pool?"

"I'd love to," Nora said. "I've been dying to learn."

"That'll make it a nice interesting game," Monty commented. He knew he could never make a decent shot until the confounded necklace was miles away.

"Then there's nothing else to do but dance," Alice decreed. "Come, Nora."

"No," Michael cried, "I'll play pool or auction or poker, I'll sit or talk or sing, but I'm hanged if I hesitate and get lost, or maxixe!"

Alice shook her head mournfully. "Ah, Michael," she said, "if you were only as light-footed as you are light-headed, what a partner you'd make. We are going to dance anyway."

Ethel hesitated at the doorway. "Aren't you dancing or playing pool, Mr. Denby?"

"In just a moment," he said. "First I have a word to say to Monty."

"I understand," she returned. "Man's god—business! Men use that excuse over the very littlest things sometimes."

"But this is a big thing," he asserted; "a two hundred thousand dollar proposition, so we're naturally a bit anxious."

Monty shook his head gravely. "Mighty anxious, believe me."

Whatever hope she might have cherished that Taylor was wrong, and this man she liked so much was innocent, faded when she heard the figure two hundred thousand dollars. That was the amount of the necklace's value, exactly. And she had wondered at Monty's strained, nervous manner. Now it became very clear that he was Denby's accomplice, dreading, and perhaps knowing as well as she, that the house was surrounded.

She told herself that the law was just, and those who disobeyed were guilty and should be punished; and that she was an instrument, impersonal, and as such, without blame. But uppermost in her mind was the thought of black treachery, of mean intriguing ways, and the certainty that this night would see the end of her friendship with the man she had sworn to deliver to the ruthless, cruel, insatiable Taylor. It was, as Taylor told her, a question of deciding between two people. She could help, indirectly, to convict a clever smuggler, or she could send her weak, dependent, innocent eighteen-year-old sister to jail. And she had said to Taylor: "I have no choice."

Denby looked at her a little puzzled. In Paris, a year ago, she had seemed a sweet, natural girl, armed with a certain dignity that would not permit men to become too friendly on short acquaintance. And here it seemed that she was almost trying to flirt with him in a wholly different way. He was not sure that her other manner was not more in keeping with the ideal he had held of her since that first meeting.

"I should be anxious, too," she said, "if I had all that money at stake. But all the same, don't be too long. I think I may ask you for that cigarette presently."

CHAPTER TEN

DENBY stood looking after her. "Bully, bully girl," he muttered.

"Anything wrong, Steve?" Monty inquired, not catching what he said.

Denby turned to the speaker slowly; his thoughts had been more pleasantly engaged.

"I don't understand why they haven't done anything," he answered. "I'm certain we were followed at the dock. When I went to send those telegrams I saw a man who seemed very much disinterested, but kept near me. I saw him again when we had our second blow-out near Jamaica. It might have been a coincidence, but I'm inclined to think they've marked us down."

"I don't believe it," Monty cried. "If they had the least idea about the necklace, they'd have pinched you at the pier, or got you on the road when it was only you and the chauffeur against their men."

Still Denby seemed dubious. "They let me in too dashed easily," he complained, "and I can't help being suspicious."

"They seemed to suspect me," Monty reminded him.

"The fellow thought you were laughing at him, that's all. They've no sense of humor," Denby returned. "What I said to-night was no fiction, Monty. Cartier's may have tipped the Customs after all."

"But you paid Harlow a thousand dollars," Monty declared.

"He wasn't the only one to know I had bought the pearls, though," Denby observed thoughtfully. "It looks fishy to me. They may have some new wrinkles in the Customs."

"That damned R. J.," Monty said viciously, "I'd like to strangle him."

"It would make things easier," Denby allowed.

"All the same," Monty remarked, "I think we've both been too fidgety."

"Dear old Monty," his friend said, smiling, "if you knew the game as I do, and had hunted men and been hunted by them as I have, you'd not blame me for being a little uneasy now."

With apprehension Monty watched him advance swiftly toward the switch on the centre wall by the window. "Get over by that window," he commanded, and Monty hurriedly obeyed him. Then he turned off the lights, leaving the room only faintly illuminated by the moonlight coming through the French windows.

"What the devil's up?" Monty asked excitedly.

"Is there anyone there on the lawn?"

Monty peered anxiously through the glass. "No," he whispered, and then added: "Yes, there's a man over there by the big oak. By Jove, there is!"

"What's he doing?" the other demanded.

"Just standing and looking over this way."

"He's detailed to watch the house. Anybody else with him?"

"Not that I can see."

"Come away, Monty," Denby called softly, and when his friend was away from observation, he switched on the light again. "Now," he asked, "do you believe that we were followed?"

"The chills are running down my spine," Monty confessed. "Gee, Steve, I hope it won't come to a gun fight."

"They won't touch you," Denby said comfortingly; "they want me."

"I don't know," Monty said doubtfully. "They'll shoot first, and then ask which is you."

Denby was unperturbed. "I think we've both been too fidgety," he quoted.

"But why don't they come in?" Monty asked apprehensively.

"They're staying out there to keep us prisoners," he was told.

"Then I hope they'll stop there," Monty exclaimed fervently.

"I can't help thinking," Denby said, knitting his brows, "that they've got someone in here on the inside, working under cover to try to get the necklace. What do you know about the butler, Lambart? Is he a new man?"

"Lord, no," Monty assured him. "He has been with Michael five years, and worships him. You'd distress Lambart immeasurably if you even hinted he'd ever handed a plate to a smuggler."

"We've got to find out who it is," Denby said decidedly, "and then, Monty, we'll have some sport."

"Then we'll have some shooting," Monty returned in disgust. "Where is that confounded necklace anyway? Is Michael carrying it around without knowing it?"

"Still in my pouch," Denby returned.

As he said this, Miss Cartwright very gently opened a door toward which his back was turned. Terrified at the thought of Taylor's possible intrusion, she had been spurred to some sort of action, and had sauntered back to the big hall with the hope of overhearing something that would aid her.

"I know they mean business," she heard Denby say, "and this is going to be a fight, Monty, and a fight to a finish."

The thought that there might presently be scenes of violence enacted in the hospitable Harrington home, scenes in which she had a definite rôle to play, which might lead even to the death of Denby as it certainly must lead to his disgrace, drove her nearly to hysteria. Taylor had inspired her with a great horror, and at the same time a great respect for his power and courage. She did not see how a man like Steven Denby could win in a contest between himself and the brutal deputy-surveyor. "Oh," she sighed, "if they were differently placed! If Steven stood for the law and Taylor for crime!"

Everything favored Taylor, it seemed to her. Denby was alone except for Monty's faltering aid, while the other had his men at hand and, above all, the protection of the law. It was impossible to regard Taylor as anything other than a victor making war on men or women and moved by nothing to pity. What other man than he would have tortured her poor little sister, she wondered.

To a woman used through the exigencies of circumstances to making her living in a business world where competition brought with it rivalries, trickeries and jealousies, the ordeal to be faced would have been almost overwhelming.

But the Cartwrights had lived a sheltered life, the typical happy family life where there is wealth, and none until to-day had ever dared to speak to Ethel as Taylor had done. She was almost frantic with the knowledge that she must play the spy, the eavesdropper, perhaps the Delilah among people who trusted her.

As she was debating what next to do, she heard Monty's voice as it seemed to her fraught with excitement and eager and quick.

"Will you have a cigarette, Dick?" she heard him call. Instantly Steven Denby wheeled about and faced the door through which she appeared to saunter languidly. Something told her that Monty had discovered her.

"Still talking business?" she said, attempting to appear wholly at ease. "I've left my fan somewhere."

"Girls are always doing that, aren't they?" Denby said pleasantly. There was no indication from his tone that he suspected she had been listening. "We'll have to find it, Monty."

"Sure, Steve, sure," Monty returned. He was not able to cloak his uneasiness.

"Steve?" the girl queried brightly. "As I came in, I thought I heard you call him 'Dick.'"

"That was our private signal," Denby returned promptly, relieving poor Monty of an answer.

"That sounds rather mysterious," she commented.

"But it's only commonplace," Denby assured her. "My favorite parlor trick is making breaks—it always has been since Monty first knew me—and invented a signal to warn me when I'm on thin ice or dangerous ground. 'Will you have a cigarette, Dick' is the one he most often uses."

"But why 'Dick?'" she asked.

"That's the signal," Denby explained. "If he said 'Steve,' I shouldn't notice it, so he always says 'Dick,' don't you, Monty?"

"Always, Steve," Monty answered quickly.

"Then you were about to make a break when I came in?" she hinted.

"I'm afraid I was," Denby admitted.

"What was it? Won't you tell me?"

"If I did," he said, "it would indeed be a break."

"Discreet man," she laughed; "I believe you were talking about me."

He did not answer for a moment but looked at her keenly. It hurt him to think that this girl, of all others, might be fencing with him to gain some knowledge of his secret. But he had lived a life in which danger was a constant element, and women ere this had sought to baffle him and betray.

He was cautious in his answer.

"You are imaginative," he said, "even about your fan. There doesn't seem to be a trace of it, and I don't think I remember your having one."

"Perhaps I didn't bring it down," she admitted, "and it may be in my room after all. May I have that promised cigarette to cheer me on my way?"

"Surely," he replied. Very eagerly she watched him take the pouch from his pocket and roll a cigarette.

Her action seemed to set Monty on edge. Suppose Denby by any chance dropped the pouch and the jewels fell out. It seemed to him that she was drawing nearer. Suppose she was the one who had been chosen to "work inside" and snatched it from him?

"Miss Cartwright," he said, and noted that she seemed startled at his voice, "can't I get your fan for you?"

"No, thanks," she returned, "you'd have to rummage, and that's a privilege I reserve only for myself."

"Here you are," Denby broke in, handing her the slim white cigarette.

She took it from him with a smile and moistened the edge of the paper as she had seen men do often enough. "You are an expert," she said admiringly.

He said no word but lighted a match and held it for her. She drew a breath of tobacco and half concealed a cough. It was plain to see that she was making a struggle to enjoy it, and plainer for the men to note that she failed.

"What deliciously mild tobacco you smoke," she cried. Suddenly she stretched out her hand for the pouch. "Do let me see."

But Denby did not pass it to her. He looked her straight in the eyes.

"I don't think a look at it would help you much," he said slowly. "The name is, in case you ever want to get any, 'without fire.'"

"What an odd name," she cried. "Without fire?"

"Yes," he answered. "You see, no smoke without fire." Without any appearance of haste he put the pouch back in his pocket.

"You don't believe in that old phrase?"

"Not a bit," he told her. "Do you?"

She turned to ascend the stairs to her room.

"No. Do make another break sometime, won't you—Dick?"

"DO MAKE ANOTHER BREAK SOMETIME, WON'T YOU—DICK?"

"I most probably shall," he retorted, "unless Monty warns me—or you."

She turned back—she was now on the first turn of the staircase. "I'll never do that. I'd rather like to see you put your foot in it—you seem so very sure of yourself—Steve." She laughed lightly as she disappeared.

Monty gripped his friend's arm tightly. "Who is that girl?"

"Why, Ethel Cartwright," he rejoined, "a close friend of our hostess. Why ask me?"

"Yes, yes," Monty said impatiently, "but what do you know about her?"

"Nothing except that she's a corker."

"You met her in Paris, didn't you?" Monty was persistent.

"Yes," his friend admitted.

"What was she doing there?"

Denby frowned. "What on earth are you driving at?"

"She was behind that door listening to us or trying to."

"So you thought that, too?" Denby cried quickly.

"Then you do suspect her of being the one they've got to work on the inside?" Monty retorted triumphantly.

"It can't be possible," Denby exclaimed, fighting to retain his faith in her. "You're dead wrong, old man. I won't believe it for a moment."

"Say, Steve," Monty cried, a light breaking in on him, "you're sweet on her."

"It isn't possible, it isn't even probable," said Denby, taking no notice of his suggestion.

"But the same idea occurred to you as did to me," Monty persisted.

"I know," Denby admitted reluctantly. "I began to be suspicious when she wanted to get hold of the pouch. You saw how mighty interested she was in it?"

"That's what startled me so," Monty told him. "But how could she know?"

"They've had a tip," Denby said, with an air of certainty, "and if she's one of 'em, she knows where the necklace was. Wouldn't it be just my rotten luck to have that girl, of all girls I've ever known, mixed up in this?"

"Old man," Monty said solemnly, "you are in love with her."

Denby looked toward the stairway by which he had seen her go.

"I know I am," he groaned.

"Oughtn't we to find out whether she's the one who's after you or not?" Monty suggested with sound good sense.

"No, we oughtn't," Denby returned. "I won't insult her by trying to trap her."

"Flub-dub," Monty scoffed. "I suspect her, and it's only fair to her to clear her of that suspicion. If she's all right, I shall be darn glad of it. If she isn't, wouldn't you rather know?"

For the first time since he had met his old school friend in Paris, Monty saw him depressed and anxious. "I don't want to have to fight her," he explained.

"I understand that," Monty went on relentlessly, "but you can't quit now—you've got to go through with it, not only for your own sake, but in fairness to the Harringtons. It would be a pretty raw deal to give them to have an exposé like that here just because of your refusal to have her tested."

"I suppose you're right," Denby sighed.

"Of course I am," Monty exclaimed.

"Very well," his friend said, "understand I'm only doing this to prove how absolutely wrong you are."

He would not admit even yet that she was plotting to betray him. Those memories of Paris were dearer to him than he had allowed himself to believe. Monty looked at him commiseratingly. He had never before seen Steven in trouble, and he judged his wound to be deeper than it seemed.

"Sure," he said. "Sure, I know, and I'll be as glad as you to find after all it's Lambart or one of the other servants. What shall we do?"

Denby pointed to the door from which Miss Cartwright had come. "Go in there," he commanded, "and keep the rest of the people from coming back here."

Monty's face fell. "How can I do that?" he asked anxiously.

"Oh, recite, make faces, imitate Irving in 'The Bells,' do anything but threaten to sing, but keep 'em there as you love me."

Obediently Monty made for the door but stopped for a moment before passing through it.

"And say, old man," he said a little hurriedly, nervous as most men are when they deal with sentiment, "don't take it too hard. Just remember what happened to Samson and Antony and Adam."

CHAPTER ELEVEN

WHEN Monty had gone, Denby took out the pouch and placed it conspicuously on the floor so that anyone descending the stairs must inevitably catch sight of it. Then, as though thinking better of it, he picked it up and placed it on one of the small tables on which was an electric shaded lamp. After looking about him for a hiding-place from which he could command a view of it and yet remain undiscovered, he decided upon a door at the left of the hall.

He had waited there only a few seconds when Ethel Cartwright's steps were heard descending.

"Oh, Mr. Denby," she called, "you were right, the fan was in my room after all." Then, as she became conscious that the room was empty, she paused and looked about her closely. Presently her eyes fell on the precious pouch so carelessly left. For a moment the excitement bereft her of ability to move. Here, only a few yards from her, was what would earn her sister's safety and her release from Taylor's power.

But she was no fool and collecting her thoughts wondered how it was possible so precious a thing could be left open to view. Perhaps it was a trap. Perhaps in the big hall behind one of its many doors or portières she was even now being watched. Denby had looked at her in a stern, odd manner, wholly different from his former way and Mr. Vaughan, of whom she had heard often enough as a pleasant, amiable fellow, had stared at her searchingly and harshly. An instinct of danger came to her aid and she glanced over to the door behind her which was slightly ajar. She remembered certainly that it was closed when she had gone upstairs for her supposititious fan.

As calmly as she could she walked to the wall and touched the bell that would summon a servant. In a few seconds Lambart entered.

"Please find Mr. Denby," she said, "and say that I am here."

Before he could turn to go, she affected to discover the leathern pouch.

"Oh, Lambart," she exclaimed, "here's Mr. Denby's tobacco; he must have forgotten it."

The man took up the pouch, assuming from her manner that she desired him to carry it to the owner. "No, I'll take it," she said, and reached for it. Lambart only saw what was to him an inexcusably clumsy gesture which dislodged it from his hand and sent it to the floor, in such a manner that it opened and the tobacco tumbled out. But the girl's gesture was cleverer than he knew for in that brief moment she had satisfied herself it was empty.

"Oh, Lambart," she said reprovingly, "how careless of you! Have you spilt it all?"

Lambart examined its interior with a butler's gravity.

"I'm afraid I have, miss," he admitted.

"I think Mr. Denby went into the library," she said, knowing that the door behind which someone—probably he—was hiding, led to that room.

Hearing her, Denby knew he must not be discovered and retreated through the empty library into a small smoking-room into which Lambart did not penetrate. The man returned to Miss Cartwright, his errand unaccomplished. "Mr. Denby is not there," he said.

"Then I will give him the pouch when I see him," she said, "and, Lambart, you need not tell him I am here."

As soon as he was gone, she ran to the window, her face no longer strained but almost joyous, and when she was assured that none watched her, lowered the curtain as a signal.

Taylor must have been close at hand, so promptly did he respond to her summons.

"Well, have you got him?" he cried sharply as he entered. "Where is he—where's the necklace?"

"You were wrong," she said triumphantly, "there is no necklace. I knew I was right."

"You're crazy," he retorted brutally.

"You said it was in the tobacco-pouch," she reminded him, "and I've searched and it isn't there at all."

"You're trying to protect him," Taylor snarled. "You're stuck on him, but you can't lie to me and get away with it."

"No, no, no," she protested. "Look, here's the very pouch, and there's no necklace in it."

"How did you get hold of it?" he snapped.

It was a moment of bitter failure for the deputy-surveyor. The sign for which he had waited patiently, and eagerly, too, despite his impassive face, was, after all, nothing but a token of disappointment. He had hoped, now that events had given him a hold over Miss Cartwright, to find her well-fitted for a sort of work that would have been peculiarly useful to his service. But her ready credulity in another man's honesty proved one of two things. Either that she lacked the intuitive knowledge to be a useful tool or else that she was deliberately trying to deceive him. But none had seen Daniel Taylor show that he realized himself in danger of being beaten.

"He left it lying on the table," she assured him eagerly.

Taylor's sneer was not pleasant to see.

"Oh, he left it on the table, did he?" he scoffed. "Well, of course there's no necklace in it then. Don't you see you've let him suspect you, and he's just trying to bluff you."

"It isn't that," she asserted. "He hasn't got it, I tell you."

"I know he has," the implacable Taylor retorted, "and you've got to find out this very night where it is. You'll probably have to search his room."

She shrank back at the very thought of it. "I couldn't," she cried. "Oh, I couldn't!"

"Yes you could, and you will," he said, in his truculent tone. "And if you land him, use the same signal, pull down the shade in his room. We'll be watching, and I've found a way to get there from the balcony."

"I can't," the girl cried in desperation. "I've done what you asked. I won't try to trap an innocent man."

He looked at her threateningly. "Oh, you won't, eh? Well, you will. I've been pretty nice to you, but I'm sick of it. You'll go through for me, and you'll go through right. I've had your sister followed—see here, look at this—" He showed her the fake warrant Duncan had prepared at his bidding. "This is a warrant for her arrest, and unless you land that necklace to-night, she'll be in the Tombs in the morning."

"Not that, not that?" she begged, covering her face with her hands.

"It's up to you," he retorted, a smile of satisfaction lighting up his face. He could see that he would be able to hold Amy's warrant over her head whenever he chose. She was beaten.

"But what can I do?" she said piteously. "What can I do?"

"I'll tell you," he said less harshly, "you're a good-looking girl; well, make use of your good looks—get around him, jolly him, get him stuck on you. Make him take you into his confidence. He'll fall for it. The wisest guys are easy when you know the way."

"Very well," she said, brightening. It seemed to her that no better way could be devised than to convince Taylor he was wrong. "I will get around him; I will get his confidence. I'll prove it to you, and I'll save him."

"But you don't have to give him your confidence, remember," Taylor warned her. "Don't give him the least tip-off, understand. If you can get him out in the garden, I'll take a chance he has the necklace on him. We'll nail him there. And don't forget," he added significantly, "that I've got a little document here with your sister's name on it. There's somebody coming," he whispered, and silently let himself out into the garden.

It was Denby who came in. "Hello," he said, "not dancing, then?"

"Hello," she said, in answer to his greeting. "I don't like dancing in August."

"I'm fortunate to find you alone," he said. "You can't imagine how delightful it is to see you again."

Her manner was particularly charming, he thought, and it gave him a pang when a suspicion of its cause passed over his mind. There had been other women who had sought to wheedle from him secrets that other men desired to know, but they were other women—and this was Ethel Cartwright.

"You don't look as though it is," she said provocatively.

He made an effort to appear as light-hearted as she.

"But I am," he assured her. "It is delightful to see you again."

"It's no more delightful than for me to see you," she returned.

"Really?" he returned. "Isn't it curious that when you like people you may not see them for a year, but when you do, you begin just where you left off."

"Where did we leave off?" she demanded with a smile.

"Why—in Paris," he said with a trace of embarrassment. "You don't want to forget our Paris, I hope?"

"Never," she cried, enthusiastically. "It was there we found that we really were congenial. We are, aren't we?"

"Congenial?" he repeated. "We're more than that—we're—"

She interrupted him. "And yet, somehow, you've changed a lot since Paris."

"For better or for worse?" he asked.

She shook her head. "For worse."

He looked at her reproachfully. "Oh, come now, Miss Cartwright, be fair!"

"In Paris you used to trust me," she said.

"And you think I don't now?" he returned.

"I'm quite sure you don't," she told him.

"Why do you say that?" Denby inquired.

"There are lots of things," she answered. "One is that when I asked you why you were here in America, you put me off with some playful excuse about being just an idler." She looked at him with a vivacious air.

"Now didn't you really come over on an important mission?"

Poor Denby, who had been telling himself that Monty's suspicions were without justification, and that this girl's good faith could not be doubted even if several circumstances were beyond his power to explain, groaned inwardly. Here she was, trying, he felt certain, to gain his confidence to satisfy the men who were even now investing the house.

But he was far from giving in yet. How could she, one of Vernon Cartwright's daughters, reared in an atmosphere wholly different from this sordid business, be engaged in trying to betray him?

"Well," he said, "suppose I did come over on something more than pleasure, what do you want to know concerning it? And why do you want to know?"

"Shall we say feminine curiosity?" she returned.

He shook his head. "I think not. There must be something more vital than a mere whim."

"Perhaps there is," she conceded, leaning forward, "I want us to be friends, really good friends; I regard it as a test of friendship. Why won't you tell me?"

He shrugged his shoulders. "Shall we say man's intuition? Oh, I know it's not supposed to be as good as a woman's, but sometimes it's much more accurate."

"So you can't trust me?" she said, steadily trying to read his thoughts.

"Can I?" he asked, gazing back at her just as steadily.

"Don't you think you can?" she fenced adroitly.

"If you do," he said meaningly.

"But aren't we friends," she asked him, "pledged that night under the moon in the Bois? You see I, too, have memories of Paris."

"Then you put it," he said quietly, "to a test of friendship."

"Yes," she answered readily.

He thought for a moment. Well, here was the opportunity to find out whether Monty was right or whether the woman he cared for was merely a spy set upon him, a woman whose kindnesses and smiles were part of her training.

"Very well," he said, "then so do I. You are right. I did not come to America idly—I came to smuggle a necklace of pearls through the Customs. I did it to-day."

The girl rose from her seat by the little table where she had sat facing him and looked at him, all the brightness gone from her face.

"You didn't, you didn't!"

"I did," he assured her.

She turned her face away from him. "Oh, I'm sorry," she wailed. "I'm sorry."

Denby looked at her keenly. He was puzzled at the manner in which she took it.

"But I fooled 'em," he boasted.

She looked about her nervously as though she feared Taylor might have listened to his frank admission and be ready to spring upon them.

"You can't tell that," she said in a lower-keyed voice. "How can you be sure they didn't suspect?"

"Because I'm comfortably settled here, and there are no detectives after me. And if there were," he confided in her triumphantly, "they'd never suspect I carry the necklace in my tobacco-pouch."

"But your pouch was empty," she cried.

"How do you know that?" he demanded quickly.

"I was here when Lambart spilt it," she explained hastily. "There it is on the mantel, I meant to have given it to you."

"I don't need it," he said, taking one similar in shape and color from his pocket.

"Two pouches!" she cried aghast. "Two?"

"An unnecessary precaution," he said carelessly, "one would have done; as it is they haven't suspected me a bit."

"You can't be certain of that," she insisted. "If they found out they'd put you in prison."

"And would you care?" he demanded.

"Why, of course I would," she responded. "Aren't we friends?"

He had that same steady look in his eyes as he asked: "Are we?"

It was a gaze she could not bring herself to meet. Assuredly, she groaned, she was not of the stuff from which the successful adventuress was made.

"Of course," she murmured in reply. "But what are you going to do?"

"I've made my plans," he told her. "I've been very careful. I've given my confidence to two people only, both of whom I trust absolutely—Monty Vaughan and"—he looked keenly at her,—"and you. I shan't be caught. I won't give in, and I'll stop at nothing, no matter what it costs, or whom it hurts. I've got to win."

It seemed to him she made an ejaculation of distress. "What is it?" he cried.

"Nothing much," she said nervously, "it's the heat, I suppose. That's why I wouldn't dance, you know. Won't you take me into the garden and we'll look at the moon—it's the same moon," she said, with a desperate air of trying to conceal from him her agitation, "that shines in Paris. It's gorgeous," she added, looking across the room where no moon was.

"Surely," he said. "It is rather stuffy indoors on a night like this." He moved leisurely over to the French windows. But she called him back. She was not yet keyed up to this supreme act of treachery.

"No, no," she called again, "don't let's go, after all."

"Why not?" he demanded, bewildered at her fitful mood.

"I don't know," she said helplessly. "But let's stay here. I'm nervous, I think."

"Nonsense," he said cheerily, trying to brace her up. "The moon is a great soother of nerves, and a friendly old chap, too. What is it?" he asked curiously. "You're miles away from here, but I don't think you're in Paris, either. It's your turn to tell me something. Where are you?"

He could not guess that her thoughts were in her home, where her poor, gentle, semi-invalid mother was probably now worrying over the sudden mood of depression which had fallen upon her younger girl. And it would be impossible for him to understand the threat of prison and disgrace which was even now hanging over Amy Cartwright's head.

"I was thinking of my sister," she told him slowly. "Come, let's go."

Before he could unfasten the French windows there was a sound of running feet outside, and Monty's nervous face was seen looking in. Nora, breathless, was hanging on to his arm.

Quickly Denby opened the doors and let the two in, and then shut the doors again. "What is it?" he demanded quickly.

"Don't go out there, Steve," Monty cried, when he could get breath enough to speak.

"Why, what is it?" Ethel Cartwright asked nervously.

"Nora and I went for a walk in the garden, and suddenly two men jumped out on us from behind the pagoda. They had almost grabbed us when one man shouted to the other fellow, 'We're wrong,' and Nora screamed and ran like the very devil, and I had to run after her of course."

"It was dreadful," said Nora gasping.

"What's dreadful?" Alice Harrington demanded, coming on the scene followed by her husband. They had been disturbed by Nora's screams.

"Won't someone please explain?" Michael asked anxiously.

"It was frightful," Nora cried.

"Let me tell it," Monty protested.

"You'll get it all wrong," his companion asserted. "I wasn't half as scared as you."

"I was talking to Nora," Monty explained, "and suddenly from the shrubbery—"

"Somebody stepped right out," Nora added.

"One at a time," Michael admonished them, "one at a time, please."

"Why, you see, Monty and I went for a walk in the garden," Nora began—

"And two men jumped out and started for us," Monty broke in.

"Great Scott," Michael cried, indignant that the privacy of his own estate should be invaded, "and here, too!"

"What did you do?" Alice asked eagerly.

"I just screamed and they ran away," Nora told her a little proudly. "Wasn't it exciting?" she added, drawing a deep breath. "Just like a book!"

"Michael," his wife said, shocked, "they might have been killed."

"What they need is a drink," he said impressively; "I'll ring for some brandy."

"I'd be all right," Monty stated emphatically, "if I could get one long breath."

"You do look a bit shaken, old man," Denby said sympathetically. "What you need is a comforting smoke. You left a pipe on the table in my room. Take my tobacco and light up."

Monty looked at the pigskin pouch as his friend handed it to him. "Gee!" he said, regarding it as one might a poisonous reptile, "I don't want that."

"That's all right," Denby said. "I can spare it. And when you're through with it, drop it in the drawer of the writing-table, will you? I always like to make myself one for coffee in the morning. I've smoked enough to-night."

By this time Monty understood what was required of him. He took the pouch respectfully and crossed toward the stairs. "I'll leave it in the drawer," he called out as he ascended the stairs.

Michael had been looking through the glass doors with a pair of binoculars. "I see nothing," he declared.

"But suppose they come back later, and break in here at night?" Alice cried.

"I shall organize the household servants and place Lambart at their head," he said gravely. "He is an excellent shot. Then there are three able-bodied men here, so that we are prepared."

"I'm sure you needn't take any such elaborate precautions," Denby told him. "No men, after once warning us, would break in here with so many servants. I imagine they were a couple of tramps who were attracted by Miss Rutledge's rings and thought they could make a quick getaway."

"This is a lesson to me to provide myself with a couple of Airedales," Michael asserted. "Things are coming to a pretty pass when one invites one's friends to come down to a week-end party and get robbed. It's worse than a hotel on the Riviera."

"Well, they didn't get anything," Nora cried. "You should have seen me run. I believe I flew, and I do believe I've lost weight!"

"But oughtn't I to go out and see?" Michael asked a little weakly.

"Certainly not," Alice commanded him firmly. "I can imagine nothing more useless than a dead husband."

He took her hand affectionately. "How right you are," he murmured gratefully. "I think, though, I ought to ask the police to keep a sharp watch."

"That's sensible," his wife agreed. "Go and telephone."

"Goodness," Nora cried suddenly, "I haven't any rings on. I must have left them on my dressing-table."

Alice looked alarmed. "And I left all sorts of things on mine. Let's go up together. And you, Ethel, have you left anything valuable about?"

"There's nothing worth taking," the girl answered.

"You look frightened to death, child," Mrs. Harrington exclaimed, as she was passing her.

Ethel sat down on the fender seat with a smile of assurance. "Oh, not a bit," she said. "There are three strong men to protect us, remember."

"Yes—two men and Michael," her hostess laughed, passing up the stairway out of view.

"The moon is still there, Miss Cartwright," Denby observed quietly. "Surely you are not tired of moons yet?"

"But those men out there," she protested.

"I'm sure they weren't after me," he returned. "They wouldn't wait in the garden, and even if they are detectives, they wouldn't get the necklace, it's safe—now."

Ethel Cartwright shook her head. "I'm afraid I've got nerves like every other woman," she confessed, "and the evening has been quite eventful enough as it is. I think I prefer to stay here."

She glanced up to see Monty descending the stairs. All this talk of robbery and actual participation in a scene of violence had induced in Monty the desire for the company of his kind.

"I thought I'd rather be down here," he stated naively.

"All right, old man," Denby said smiling. "Glad to have you. Did you put the pouch where I said?"

"Yes," Monty answered, handing him a key, "and I locked it up," he explained.

"Good!" his friend exclaimed, putting the key in his pocket.

Miss Cartwright yawned daintily. "Excitement seems to make me sleepy," she said. "I think I shall go."

"You're not going to leave us yet?" Denby said reproachfully.

"I was up very early," she told him.

"I guess everything is safe now," Monty assured her.

"Let's hope so," Denby said. "Still, the night isn't half over yet. Pleasant dreams, Miss Cartwright."

She paused on the half landing and looked down at the two men.

"I'm afraid they won't be quite—that."

Monty crept to the foot of the stairway and made certain she was passed out of hearing. "Steve," he said earnestly, "she's gone now to get into your room."

"No, she hasn't," Denby protested, knowing he was lying.

Monty looked at his friend in wonderment. Usually Denby was quick of observation, but now he seemed uncommonly dull.

"Why, she never made a move to leave until she knew I'd put the pouch in the drawer. Then she said she was tired and wanted to go to bed. You must have noticed how she took in everything you said. She's even taken to watching me, too. What makes you so blind, Steve?"

"I'm not blind," Denby said, a trifle irritably. "It happens you are magnifying things, till everything you see is wrong."

"Nonsense," Monty returned bluntly. "If she gets that necklace it's all up with us, and you needn't pretend otherwise."

"Make your mind easy," Denby exclaimed, "she won't get it."

"May I ask what's going to stop her?" Monty inquired, goaded into sarcasm. "Do you think she needs to know the combination of an ordinary lock like that top drawer?"

"The necklace isn't there," Denby said.

Monty looked at him piteously. "For Heaven's sake don't tell me I've got it somewhere on me!"

Denby drew it out of a false pocket under the right lapel of his coat and held the precious string up to the other's view. "That's why," he observed.

"Then everything's all right," Monty cried with unrestrained joy.

"Everything's all wrong," Denby corrected.

"But, Steve," Monty said reproachfully, "the necklace—"

"Oh, damn the necklace!" Denby interrupted viciously.

Monty shook his head mournfully. His friend's aberrations were astounding.

"Steve," he said slowly, "you're a fool!"

"I guess I am," the other admitted. "But," he added, snapping his teeth together, "I'm not such a fool as to get caught, Monty, so pull yourself together, something's bound to happen before long."

"That's what I'm afraid of," sighed Monty.

CHAPTER TWELVE

ON the way to her room Ethel Cartwright met Michael Harrington, a box of cigars in his hand, coming toward the head of the stairway.

"Whither away?" he demanded.

"To bed," she returned. "The excitement's been too much for me."

"This box," he said, lovingly caressing it, "contains what I think are the best that can be smoked." He opened and showed what seemed to her cigars of a very large size. "I'm going to give the boys one apiece as a reward for bravery." He laughed with glee. "And as Lambart is going to be one of the search party, I'm going to give him one, too. He'll either leave at my temerity in offering him the same kind of weed his employer smokes, or else he'll have it framed."

"A search party?" she said. "What do you mean?"

"We're going to beat the bushes for tramps," he said. "I am directing operations from the balcony outside my room. The general in command," he explained, "never gets on the firing-line in modern warfare."

"Is Mr. Denby going?" she asked.

"No, no," he said. "I can't expect my guests to expose themselves to the risk of being shot. Don't you be alarmed," he said solicitously, "I shall be at hand in case of trouble."

When she reached her room she sat motionless for a few moments on the edge of the bed. Then suddenly, she rose and walked along a corridor and knocked at the door of the room she knew was Alice Harrington's.

"Alice," she said nervously, and there was no doubt in the elder woman's mind that the girl was thoroughly upset, "I'm nervous of sleeping in the room you've given me. Can't I sleep somewhere near people? Let me have that room I had the last time I was here."

"Why, my dear girl, of course, if you want it," Alice said sympathetically. "But it isn't as pretty, and I especially had this bigger room for you. Don't be a silly little girl; you'll be asleep in five minutes. Better still, I'll come and read till you're drowsy."

"Please humor me," the other pleaded. "I'd rather be where, if I scream, someone can hear, and the men are sleeping down there, and one after all does depend on them in emergencies."

"All right," Alice said good-humoredly, "I'll ring for the servants to take your things in."

"We can do it," Ethel said eagerly. "I've only one cabin trunk, and it weighs nothing. Why disturb them?"

When they had moved the baggage down the halls to the smaller room, there was no key to lock the door which led to a connecting room.

"Whose is that?" Ethel demanded.

"Mr. Denby's," she was told. "I always give men big rooms, because they're so untidy. Michael will know where the key is. He has every one of the hundred keys with a neat label on it. He's so methodical in some things. By the time you're ready for bed I'll have it."

A few minutes later the intervening door was safely locked and Mrs. Harrington had left the girl, feeling that perhaps she, too, would be nervous if she had not her Michael close at hand.

Directly the girl was alone she sprang out of bed and hurriedly put on a white silk negligée. So far her plans had prospered admirably. The bedroom from which she had moved was so situated that if she were to undertake the search of Denby's room, she must pass the rooms of her host and hostess and also that of Nora Rutledge. And this search was imperative. Out in the darkness Taylor and his men were waiting impatiently. Presently a band of men, armed in all probability, would sally forth from the house and might just as likely capture the Customs officers. Supposing Taylor took this as treachery on her part and denounced her before the Harringtons? Nothing would save Amy then.

If only she could discover the necklace and give the signal in time so that the deputy-surveyor could come legitimately into the house! She told herself that she must control this growing nervousness; that her movements must be swift and sure, and that she must banish all thought of the man she had met in Paris, or the punishment that would be his.

Fortunately his guests could not escape Michael and his big cigars; and cigars, as she knew from her father's use of them, are not consumed as a cigarette may be and thrown quickly away.

The key turned in the lock stiffly and it seemed to her, waiting breathless, that the sound must be audible everywhere. But as quiet still ruled outside in the corridors, she pushed the door half-open and peered into the room. It was dark save for the moonlight, but she could see to make her way to a writing-table, on which was an electric lamp.

She turned it on and then looked about her nervously. It was a large, well-furnished room, and to the right of her a big alcove with a bed in it. There was a large French window leading to the balcony which Taylor had noted and proposed to use if she were successful in her search.

She did not dare to look out, for fear the search party might see her, so she centered her attention upon the locked drawer in which the necklace was awaiting her. There was a brass paper-knife lying on the table, heavy enough she judged, to pry open any ordinary lock. Very cautiously she set about her work. It called for more strength than she had supposed, but the lock seemed to be yielding gradually when there fell upon her anxious ear sounds of footsteps coming down the corridor.

She sprang to her feet and listened intently, and was satisfied herself that she was in imminent danger. Putting out the light she turned to run to her room, and in doing so knocked the paper-knife to the floor. To her excited fancy it clattered hideously as it fell, but she reached her room safely and locked the door.

She was hardly in shelter before Denby came into his room and switched on the light. He was still smoking the first third of his host's famous cigar. He sauntered to the window and looked over the lawn and wondered what luck the searchers would have. He had permitted himself to be urged by Harrington to a course of inactivity. It was not his wish to be brought face to face with his enemy while he had the jewels in a place they would instantly detect. He took the pearls from their hiding-place and threw them carelessly on the table. Then seeing the paper-knife on the floor he stooped to pick it up. But lying near it were little splinters of white wood that instantly arrested his attention. He knelt down, lit a match, and examined them without disturbing them in any way. And then his eyes travelled upward, until the scratches by the lock were plain.

Experience told him plainly that the drawer had been attempted and that recently, in fact, within a half-hour since Monty had placed his pouch there with the pearls as he supposed in it.

While he was standing there motionless, sounds in the hall outside disturbed him. Presently a knock sounded on the door. Before answering he picked up the pearls and placed them in his pocket. Then he called out: "Who is it?"

"It's me," came Monty's voice in answer.

"Come in," he called.

Monty entered nervously. "Everything all right?" he demanded.

"Yes," his friend said, and then looked at him. Monty's appearance was slightly dishevelled. "What's happened?" he asked.

Monty ignored the question. "I was afraid everything might be all wrong," he cried. "This is the first time I've been able to swallow comfortably for an hour. I thought my heart was permanently dislocated."

"What's been happening downstairs?" Denby inquired.

"Nothing," Monty told him, "and it's the limit to have nothing happen."

"I thought Harrington was organizing a search party."

"Oh, we searched," Monty admitted. "I was nominally in charge, but Lambart was the directing genius. He was an officer's orderly in his youth and is some tactician, believe me." Monty pointed to his muddied knees. "He stretched clothes-lines over the paths to catch the tramps, and I was the first victim. We looked everywhere, all of us, Lambart, the under-butler, two chauffeurs and I, and we didn't even flush a cat."

"That's odd," his listener commented. "They'll be back. They're not frightened away by you fellows with lanterns. They'll be back."

"I bet they will," Monty grumbled, "and with the militia."

"Don't lose your nerve now, old man," Denby counselled.

"I wish I could," Monty cried. "This certainly is getting on it. It's a lesson not to get discontented with my lot. I've got that creepy feeling all the time that they're coming closer to us."

"But that's the real sport of it," Denby pointed out.

"Sport be damned," he said crossly. "Your ideas about foxes and mine don't coincide. I don't think he likes being hunted. And at that he's got something on us; he knows who's chasing him."

"So shall we soon," he was reminded.

"Yes," Monty grumbled, "when we're shot full of holes."

"Don't be afraid of getting shot at," Denby said smiling. "You amateurs have no idea how few shots hit the mark even at short range. I've been shot at three times and I've not a scar to show."

"Job must be your favorite author," Monty commented sourly. "I hate the noise. I'm scared to death; I thought I wanted excitement, but life on a farm for me hereafter."

"But, my dear boy," Denby said more seriously, "you are not in this. They're after me and this." He held up the necklace. "You're a spectator merely."

"Rot!" Monty cried. "I'm what they call an accessory and if you think I'm going to clear out now, all I can say is you ought to know me better than that. I want to be doing something; it's the talking that gets on my nerves. They'll be here soon, you may bet on that. They're going to search this room."

"Somebody's done that already," he was told.

"Who?" Monty cried anxiously. "That girl?"

"I think not. Her room is in the other wing, as I found out indirectly. To come here she'd have to run an awful risk. If she comes it will be later, when everyone is asleep."

"Then who could it have been?" Monty demanded. He turned suddenly on his heel.

There was someone even now listening at the door. Then there was a faint, discreet knock. He dropped into the nearest chair and looked at the other man with a blanched face.

"Pinched!" he cried.

"Hsh!" the other commanded softly, and then louder: "Come in."

The smiling face of Michael Harrington beamed upon them. In his hands he carried a tray whereon two generous highballs reposed.

"Hello, boys," he cried genially, "I've brought up those two nightcaps I promised you. Nothing like 'em after excitement such as we've had."

"You never looked so good to me, Michael," Monty cried affectionately.

"Now, Denby," Michael said, handing him the glass in Lambart's best manner.

"Thanks, all the same," his guest returned, "but I don't think I will—not yet at any rate."

"Good!" Michael cried. "Luck's with me." He drained the glass with the deepest satisfaction. "Ah, that was needed. Now, Monty, after your exertions you won't disappoint me?"

"Not for me, either," Monty exclaimed.

"Splendid," said the gratified Michael. "At your age I would have refused it absolutely." He looked at the glass affectionately. "I'll take the encore in a few minutes. Alice does cut me down so dreadfully. Just one light one before dinner—mostly Vermouth—and one drink afterward. I welcome any extra excitement like this."

"Aren't you master in your own house?" Denby asked smiling. He had fathomed the secret of the happy relations of his host and hostess, and was not deceived by Harrington when he represented himself the sport of circumstances.

"You bet I'm not," said Michael, without resentment. "By the way," he added, "if you want your nightcaps later, ring for Lambart. He's used to being summoned at any hour."

"I won't forget," Denby returned.

"I hope you won't," his host assured him. "I'd hate to think of Lambart having a really good night's rest." He pointed to an alarm on the wall by the door. "But don't get up half asleep and push that red thing over there."

"What on earth is it?" Monty asked. "It looks like a hotel fire-alarm—'Break the glass in case of fire.'"

"It's a burglar-alarm that wakes the whole house."

"What?" Denby cried, suddenly interested. "You don't really expect burglars?"

"I know it's funny," Michael said, "and a bit old maidish, but I happen to be vice-president of the New York Burglar Insurance Company, and I've got to have their beastly patents in the house to show my faith in 'em."

"I'll keep away from it," Denby assured him, looking at it curiously.

"The last man who had this room sent it off by mistake. Said a mosquito worried him so much that he threw a shoe at it. He missed the mosquito—between you and me," Michael said confidentially, "we haven't any out here at Westbury—but he hit the alarm. I'm afraid Hazen had been putting too many nightcaps on his head and couldn't see straight. Mrs. Harrington made me search the whole house. Of course there wasn't anyone there and Alice seemed sorry that I'd had my hunt in vain. The beauty of these things," the vice-president commented, "is that they warn the burglars to get out and so you don't get shot as you might if you hadn't told 'em you were coming."

Michael took up the second glass and had barely taken a sip when quick, light footfalls approached.

"Good Lord," said he, "my wife! Here, Monty, quick," placing the half-emptied glass in Denby's hand and the one from which he had first drunk in Monty's, "I count on you, boys," he whispered, and then strode to the door and flung it open.

"Are we intruders?" his wife asked.

"You are delightfully welcome," Denby cried. "Please come in."

"We thought you'd still be up," Nora explained. "Michael said he was bringing you up some highballs."

"Great stuff," Monty said, taking his cue, "best whiskey I ever tasted. Nothing like really old Bourbon after all."

Michael shot a glance of agonized reproach at the man who could make such a stupid mistake. "Monty," he explained to his wife, who had caught this ingenuous remark and had looked at him inquiringly, "is still so filled with excitement that he doesn't know old Scotch when he tastes it."

"Your husband is a noble abstainer," Denby said quickly, to help them out, "we place temptation right before him and he resists."

"That's my wife's training," said Harrington, smiling complacently.

"I'm not so sure," she returned. "Putting temptation before Michael, Mr. Denby, shows him just like old Adam—only Michael's weakness is for grapes, not apples."

"We've come," Nora reminded them, "to get a fourth at auction. We're all too much excited to sleep. Mr. Denby, I'm sure you're a wonderful player. Surely you must shine at something."

"Among my other deficiencies," he confessed, "I don't play bridge."

Nora sighed. "There remains only Monty. Monty," she commanded, "you must play."

"Glad to!" he cried. "I like company, and I'm not tired either."

Suddenly he caught sight of Denby's face. His look plainly said, "Refuse."

"In just a few minutes," Monty stammered. "I was just figuring out something when you came in. How long will it take, Steve?"

"Hardly five minutes," Denby said.

"It's a gold-mine you see," Monty explained laboriously, "and first it goes up, and then it goes down."

"I always strike an average," Michael told him. "It's the easiest way."

"Is it a good investment?" Alice demanded. She had a liking for taking small flutters with gold-mines.

"You wouldn't know one if you saw it," her husband said, laughing.

"I learnt what I know from you," she reminded him.

"I'd rather dance than bridge it," Nora said impatiently, doing some rather elaborate maxixe steps very gracefully and humming a popular tune meanwhile.

"Be quiet," Alice warned her; "you'll disturb Ethel."

"Has Miss Cartwright gone to bed?" Denby asked her.

"She felt very tired," Alice explained.

"It's wrong to go to bed so early," Nora exclaimed. "It can't be much after two."

She sang a few bars of another song much in vogue, but Alice stopped her again.

"Hush, Nora, don't you understand Ethel's in the next room asleep, or trying to?"

"I thought it was empty," Nora said, in excuse for her burst of song.

"Ethel insisted on changing. She was very nervous and she wanted to be down near the men in case of trouble."

"And I had to go through forty-seven bunches of keys to get one to fit that door," her husband complained. Denby shot a swift glance toward Monty, who was wearing an "I told you so" expression. "She seemed positively afraid of you, Denby, from what my wife said," Harrington concluded.

"You're not drinking your highball, Mr. Denby," Alice observed.

"I'm saving it," he smiled.

"That's a very obvious hint," Nora cried. "Let's leave them, Alice." She sauntered to the door.

"Very well," her hostess said, "and we'll expect you in a few minutes, Monty. You're coming, Michael?"

"In just a moment," he returned. "I've got one more old wheeze I want to spring on Denby. He's a capital audience for the elderly ones."

"When Mr. Denby has recovered," she commanded, "come down and play."

"Certainly, my dear," he said obediently.

"And, Michael," she said smiling, "don't think you've fooled me."

"Fooled you," he exclaimed innocently, "why, I'd never even dream of trying to!"

His wife moved toward Denby and took the half-finished highball from his hand.

"Michael," she said, handing it to him, "here's the rest of your drink."

She went from the room still smiling at the deep knowledge she had of her Michael's little ways.

Michael imbibed it gratefully.

"My wife's a damned clever woman," he exclaimed enthusiastically, as he trotted out obediently in her wake.

Directly he had gone Denby went quickly to the door and made sure it was closed tightly. "It was that girl, after all, Monty!" he said in a low, tense voice. "She tried to pry open the drawer with that paper-knife. You can see the marks. I found the knife on the floor, where she'd dropped it on hearing me at the door."

Monty looked at him with sympathy in his eyes. "That's pretty tough, old man," he said softly.

"It's hard to believe that she is the kind of woman to take advantage of our friendship to turn me over to the police," he admitted. Then his face took on a harder, sterner look. "But it's no use beating about the bush; that's exactly what she did."

"I'm sorry, mighty sorry," Monty said, realizing as he had never done what this perfidy meant to his old friend.

"I don't want to have to fight her," Denby said. "The very idea seems unspeakable."

"What can we do if you don't?" Monty asked doubtfully.

"If she'll only tell me who it is that sent her here—the man who's after me—I'll fight him, and leave her out of it."

"But if she won't do that?" Monty questioned.

"Then I'll play her own game," Denby answered, "only this time she follows my rules for it." As he said this both of the men fancied they could hear a creaking in the next room.

"What's that?" Monty demanded.

Denby motioned to him to remain silent, and then tiptoed his way to the door connecting the rooms.

"Is she there?" Monty felt himself compelled to whisper.

Denby nodded acquiescence and quietly withdrew to the centre of the room.

"Has she heard us?" asked his friend.

"I don't think so. I heard her close the window and then come over to the door."

He crossed to the desk and began to write very fast.

"What are you doing?" Monty inquired softly.

Denby, scribbling on, did not immediately answer him. Presently he handed the written page to Monty. "Here's my plan," he said, "read it."

While Monty was studying the paper Denby moved over to the light switch, and the room, except for the rose-shaded electric lamp, was in darkness.

"Jumping Jupiter!" Monty exclaimed, looking up from the paper with knit brows.

"Do you understand?" Denby asked.

"Yes," Monty answered agitatedly; "I understand, but suppose I get rattled and make a mistake when the time comes?"

"You won't," Denby replied, still in low tone. "I'm depending on you, Monty, and I know you won't disappoint me." When he next spoke it was in a louder voice, louder in fact than he needed for conversational use.

"It's a pity Miss Cartwright has gone to bed," he exclaimed. "I might have risked trying to learn bridge, if she'd been willing to teach me. She's a bully girl."

"Don't talk so loud," Monty advised him, grinning.

"In these dictagraph days the walls have ears. Let's go outside. We can't tell who might hear us in this room. We'll be safe enough on the lawn."

"A good idea," Denby agreed, moving away from the connecting door which they guessed had a listener concealed behind it, and turning out the lights. And Ethel Cartwright, straining her ears, heard the door opened and banged noisily, and footsteps hurrying past toward the stairway. It was at last the opportunity.

CHAPTER THIRTEEN

SHE turned the key, less noisily this time, and stepped into Denby's room. Making her way to the drawer she gave it a gentle pull. But it was still fastened, and she grasped the heavy brass knife when of a sudden the room was full of light, and Denby stepped from the shadow of the door where he had been concealed.

"Oh!" she cried in terror, and turned her face away from him.

He walked slowly over to the table by which she stood.

"So you've come for the necklace, then? Why do you want it?"

She looked at him in desperation. Only the truth would serve her now.

"I am employed by the government. I was sent here to get it," she answered.

"What?" he cried. "The charming Miss Cartwright a secret service agent! It's quite incredible."

"But it's true," she said.

"Who employed you?" he asked sharply.

"I can't tell you that," she said slowly.

"Then how can I believe you?" he asked her.

"But it's the truth," she insisted. "For what other reason should I be here?"

"Women have collected jewels before now for themselves as well as their governments," he reminded her.

She flushed. "Do you wish to insult me?"

"I don't think you quite realize your position," he said. "I find you here trying to steal something of mine. If you tell me the name of the man, or men, under whose orders you are acting, I may be able to believe."

"I can't tell you," she cried; "I can't tell you."

"It's most likely to be Bangs," he said meditatively, and then turned to her quickly. "It was John H. Bangs of the secret service who sent you."

At all costs she knew she must keep the name of Daniel Taylor from him. To admit that it was a fellow official would do no harm.

"Yes," she said; "it was."

Contempt looked from his face. "You lie, Miss Cartwright, you lie!"

"Mr. Denby!" she cried.

"I've no time for politeness now," he told her. "There is no Bangs in the secret service."

"But you, how can you know?" she said, fighting for time.

"It's my business to know my opponents," he observed. "Can't you tell the truth?"

"I can't tell you who it was," she persisted, "but if you'll just give me the necklace—"

He laughed scornfully at her childish request. Her manner puzzled him extremely. He had seen her fence and cross-examine, use her tongue with the adroitness of an old hand at intrigue, and yet she was simple, guileless enough to ask him to hand over the necklace.

"And if I refuse you'll call the men in who seized Mr. Vaughan, thinking it was I, and let them get the right man this time?"

"I don't know," she said despairingly. "What else can I do? I can't fail."

"Nor can I," he snapped, "and don't intend to, either. Do you know what happens to a man who smuggles in the sort of thing I did and resists the officials as I shall do, and is finally caught? I've seen it, and I know. It's prison, Miss Cartwright, and gray walls and iron bars. It means being herded for a term of years with another order of men, the men who are crooked at heart; it means the losing of all one's hopes in prison gloom and coming out debased and suspected by every man set in authority over you, for evermore. I've sometimes gone sick at seeing men who have done as I am doing, but have not escaped. I'm not going to prison, Miss Cartwright, remember that."

"But I don't want you to," she cried eagerly, so eagerly, that he groaned to think her magnificent acting should be devoted to such a scene as this. "I don't want you to."

"Then there's only one way out of it for both of us," he said, coming nearer.

"What?" she asked fervently.

"Tell them you've failed, that you couldn't find it anywhere."

"I couldn't," she said vehemently.

There was a certain studied contempt in his manner which hurt her badly. And to know that he would always regard her as an adventuress, unprincipled and ready to sell herself for the rewards of espionage, and never have even one pleasant and genuine memory of her, made her desperate.

"I didn't intend you to lose on the transaction," he said coldly. "I'll give you ten thousand dollars."

"Oh, no, no!" she cried, "you don't understand."

"Twenty thousand, then," he said. "Only you and I would know. Your principals could never hold it against you. Isn't it a good offer?"

She made a gesture of despair. "It's no good."

"Twenty thousand no good!" he jeered. "Think again, Miss Cartwright. It will pay you better to stand in with me than give me up."

"No, no!" she cried, half hysterically.

"It's all I can afford," he said. Her manner seemed so strange, that for the first time since he had found her in his room, he began to doubt whether, after all, it was merely the splendid acting he had supposed.

"I can't accept," she told him. "I've *got* to get that necklace; it means more than any money to me."

He looked at her keenly, seeking to gauge the depth of her emotion.

"Then they've got some hold on you," he asserted.

"No," she assured him, "I must get the necklace."

"So you're going to make me fight you then?" he questioned.

"I've got to fight," she exclaimed.

"Look here," he said, after a moment's pause, "let's get this thing right. You won't accept any—shall we call it compromise?—and you won't tell me for whom you are acting. And you won't admit that you are doing this because someone has such a hold on you that you must obey. Is that right, so far?"

For a moment she had a wild idea of telling him, of putting an end to the scene that was straining her almost to breaking-point. She knew he could be chivalrous and tender, and she judged he could be ruthless and hard if necessity compelled. But above all, and even stronger than her fear of irrevocably breaking with him and being judged hereafter as one unworthy, was the dread of Taylor and that warrant that could at his will send Amy to prison and her mother possibly to her grave. She hardened herself to go through with the ordeal.

"So far you are right," she admitted.

"Then it remains only for us two to fight. I hate fighting women. A few hours ago I would have sworn that you and I never could fight, but a few hours have shown me that I'm as liable to misread people as—as Monty, for example. You say you've got to fight. Very well then; I accept the challenge, and invite you to witness my first shot."

He walked to the door through which she had come and opening it, took the key from her side of it, locked it, and put the key in his pocket.

"What do you mean?" she cried.

"Merely that I'm going to keep you here," he retorted. "I was afraid we might be interrupted."

"Open that door!" she commanded quickly.

"When I am ready no doubt I shall," he returned.

"You wouldn't do that?" she cried, beginning to realize that she was to have no easy victory if indeed victory were to be her reward.

"I regret the necessity," he said. "These methods don't particularly appeal to me, but we have declared war, and there's no choice."

"But I don't understand," she said nervously.

"Don't you?" he said, coming nearer and looking at her closely. "Don't you understand that you are a beautiful woman and I am a man? Have you forgotten that it's nearly three, and you are in my room, the room next which you begged to be moved? They were a little puzzled at your wanting that key so badly, and when you're found here *en negligée*—for you will be found here—I think I know the world well enough to judge what construction will be placed upon that discovery."

For the moment she forgot about everything but the personal aspect of the situation in which she found herself. That this man of all others should be willing to compromise her reputation awakened the bitterest contempt for him.

"I thought at least *you* were a *man*!" she cried.

"I am," he returned without heat. "That's just it, Miss Cartwright, I'm a man, and you are a woman."

"And I thought you were my friend," she exclaimed indignantly.

"Please don't bandy the name of friendship with me," he said with a sneer. "You of all women that live, to dare to talk like that! You knew I liked you—liked you very much, and because you were so sure of it, you wheedled me into betraying myself. You smiled and lied and pledged our friendship, and called to mind those days in Paris, which were the happiest recollections of all my life. And yet it was all done so that you might get enough out of me to lead me, with a prison sentence awaiting me, to the man who gives you your orders." He took a few swift paces up and down the room. "This indignation of yours is a false note. We'll keep to the main facts. You are sworn to betray me, and I am sworn to defeat you."

"Don't think that," she said wretchedly; "I wasn't—"

"And when I told you the truth," he went on inexorably, "you asked me to go into the garden where they were waiting for me."

"I couldn't help it," she said, as calmly as she was able.

"And when you thought I was sending the necklace here you trumped up a flimsy excuse so that you might be able to steal in here and get it. Is that sort of thing in your code of friendship?"

"I wasn't trying to trap you," she explained. "I thought you were innocent, and I wanted to convince them of it, too."

"No doubt," he said tauntingly, "and when you found out I was guilty, you still tried to save me, I suppose, by asking me to walk into their trap?"

The girl made an effort to defend her course of action. She knew that without the admission of the truth he must feel his point of view unassailable, but she wanted him not to think too hardly of her.

"After all," she declared, "you had broken the law. You are guilty. Why should my behavior be so called into account?"

"It isn't that at all," he returned impatiently. "You didn't play the game fairly. You used a woman's last weapon—her sex. Well, I can play your game, too, and I will. You shall stay here till morning."

"You don't dare to keep me!" she cried.

"Oh, yes, I do," he retorted easily.

She assumed as well as she could an air of bravado, a false air of courage that might convince him she was not so easily frightened as she felt.

"And you think the possible loss of my reputation is going to frighten me into letting you go?"

"I do," he said readily.

"Well, you're wrong," she assured him, "I have only to tell them the truth about the necklace and what I'm doing here—"

"But the truth is so seldom believed," he reminded her, "especially when you've no evidence to support it. A lie is a much more easily digested morsel."

"All the evidence I need," she asserted, "is in that locked drawer."

"Quite so," he admitted. "I'd forgotten that, only it happens you're wrong again." He drew the necklace from his pocket and showed it to her. "It's a beauty, isn't it?"

Moving over to the table he scribbled a few words on a sheet of paper.

"What are you doing?" she asked.

"Manufacturing evidence," he returned calmly.

"Meanwhile," she said, gathering courage, "I propose to leave this room."

"An excellent idea from your way of thinking," he said, looking up. "Naturally I'm interested to know how."

"I'll show you," she responded, and moved quickly to the bell button which she pushed violently. "Now, Mr. Denby," she cried triumphantly. "This is my first shot! When the servants come, I shall take the necklace with me."

She was disappointed to see no trace of alarm on his face. Instead, he answered her calmly enough.

"What a pity you did that—you'll regret it so very soon."

"Shall I?" she said satirically, and watched him go to the window. As he did so, a low whistle was heard coming from the lawn beneath. Then he took the necklace, wrapped it in the note he had written, and tossed it through the opening.

"I hardly think you'll take it with you," he observed suavely.

"I shall get it," she returned. "I shall tell the Harringtons exactly what you are, and that you threw it on the lawn."

"Wrong again, Miss Cartwright," he said patiently. "If you'll stand where I am, you will see the retreating figure of my friend Monty, who has it with him. Monty managed rather well, I think. His whistle announced the coast was clear."

"But he can't get away with those men out there," she reminded him.

"Monty waited until they were gone," he repeated. "For the moment, your friends of the secret service have left us."

"Then I'll tell Mr. Harrington about Monty, that he's your accomplice."

He shook his head. "I hardly think they'd believe that even from you. That Montague Vaughan, whose income is what he desires it to be, should lower himself to help me, is one of the truthful things nobody could possibly credit. If you could ring in some poor but honest young man it would sound so much more probable, but Monty, no."

She looked at him like a thing stricken. Her poor bravado fell from her. She felt beaten, and dreaded to think what might be the price of her failure.

"And since you forced me," he added, "I've had to play my last card. The note that I threw to Monty was a letter to you. He'll leave it where it can easily be found."

"A letter to me!" she repeated.

"It contained a suggestion that you try to get the room next mine, pleading nervousness, and come here to-night. It was the invitation—of a lover."

"You beast!" she cried, flaming out into rage. "You coward!"

"You had your warning," he reminded her. "The note will be conclusive, and no matter what you say, you will find yourself prejudged. It's the world's way to prejudge. The servants don't seem to be coming, and you'll be found here in the morning. What explanation will you have to offer?" He waited for her to speak, but she made no answer.

"I think the episode of the necklace remains as between just you and me," he added slowly, watching her closely.

"The servants will come," she cried. "I shan't have to stay here."

"If they disappoint you," he remarked, "may I suggest that burglar-alarm? It will wake everybody up, the Harringtons, Miss Rutledge, and all, even if they're in bed and asleep soundly. Why don't you ring it? Miss Cartwright, I *dare* you to ring it!"

Just then there came the sounds of footsteps in the corridor, then a knock at the door. Denby waited calmly for some word from the girl. The knock was repeated.

"Well," he whispered at last, "why don't you answer?"

She shrank back. "No, no, I can't."

Denby moved to the door. "Who is it?" he asked.

Lambart's respectful voice made answer: "You rang, sir?"

"Yes," he returned, "I forgot to tell you that Miss Cartwright wished to be called at seven. Call me at the same time, too. That's all, Lambart; sorry to have had to disturb you. Good-night."

He stood listening until the man's footsteps died away. Then he turned, and came toward the girl.

"So you didn't dare denounce me after all," he said mockingly.

"Oh, I knew it was all a joke," she said, with an attempt to pass it over lightly. "I knew you couldn't be so contemptible."

"A joke!" he exclaimed grimly. "Why does it seem a joke?"

"If you'd meant what you'd said, you'd have called Lambart in. That would have answered your purpose very well. But I knew that you'd never do that. I knew you couldn't."

"I'm afraid I shall have less faith hereafter in woman's intuition," he returned. "I can keep you here, and I will. No other course is open to me." A clock outside struck. "It's just three," he observed. "In four hours' time a maid will go to your room and find it empty. It's a long time till then, so why not make yourself as comfortable as you can? Please sit down."

The girl sank into a chair more because she was suddenly conscious of her physical weakness than for the reason he offered it her in mocking courtesy.

"I can't face it," she cried hysterically; "the disgrace and humiliation! I can't face it!"

"You've got to face it," he said sternly.

"I can't," she repeated. "It's horrible, it's unfair—if you'll let me go, I'll promise you I won't betray you."

"You daren't keep silent about me," he answered. "How can I let you go?"

"I'm telling you the truth," she said simply.

"Then tell me who sent you here," he entreated her. "You know what it means to me; you can guess what it means to you. If you tell me, it may save us both."

"I can't!" she cried. "I can't! Oh, please, please!"

He took her in his arms, roughly, exasperated by her denial.

"By God, I'll make you tell!" he said angrily.

"Don't touch me," she said shuddering.

"Who sent you here?" he demanded, not releasing her.

"I'm afraid," she groaned. "Oh, I'm afraid. I hate you! I hate you! Let me go! let me go!"

"Who sent you here?" he repeated, still holding her.

"I'll tell," she said brokenly. Then, when he let her go, she sank into a chair. "I can't go through with it—you've beaten me—Oh, I tried so hard, so hard, but you've won. It's too unfair when it's not my fault. You can't understand, or you wouldn't spoil my whole life like this. It's not only me, it's my mother, my sister—Amy."

Denby, watching her hardly controllable agitation, was forced to readjust his opinion concerning her. This was not any adventuress trained in artifice and ruse, but the woman he had thought her to be in the deepest sorrow. The bringing in of her mother and sister was not, he felt sure, a device employed merely to gain his sympathy and induce leniency in her captor.

And when it seemed she must sob out a confession of those complex motives which had led her to seek his betrayal, Denby saw her clench her hands and pull herself together.

"No," she said, rising to her feet, her weakness cast off, "I won't quit—no matter what happens to me. I'll expose you, and tell them everything. I'll let them decide between us—whether they'll believe you or me. It's either you or my sister, and I'll save her."

He was now more than ever certain he was stumbling upon something which would bring him the blessed assurance that she had not sold herself for reward.

"Your sister?" he cried eagerly.

"They shan't send her to prison," the girl said doggedly.

"You're doing all this to save your sister from prison?" he asked her gently.

"She depends on me so," she answered dully. "They shan't take her."

"Then you've been forced into this?" he asked. "You haven't done it of your own free will?"

"No, no," she returned, "but what else could I do? She was my little sister; she came first."

"And you weren't lying to me—trying to trick me for money?"

"Can't you see," she said piteously, "that I wanted to save you, too, and wanted you to get away? I said you were innocent, but they wouldn't believe me and said I had to go on or else they'd send Amy to prison. They have a warrant all ready for her in case I fail. That's why I'm here. Oh, please, please, let me go."

Steven Denby looked into her eyes and made his resolve. "You don't know how much I want to believe in you," he exclaimed. "It may spoil everything I've built on, but I'm going to take the chance." He unlocked the door that led to her room. "You can go, Miss Cartwright!"

"Oh, you are a man, after all," she cried, deep gratitude in her voice, and a relief at her heart she could as yet scarcely comprehend. And as she made to pass him she was startled by a shrill sharp whistle outside.

"The devil!" he cried anxiously, and ran to the window.

"What is it?" she called, frightened. It was not the low whistle that Monty had used, but a menacing, thrilling sound.

"Your friends of the secret service have come back," he answered, "but they mustn't see us together." Quickly he lowered the window-shade, and stepped back to the centre of the room, coming to a sudden pause as he saw the terror on the girl's face.

"Oh, my God," she screamed, "what have you done? That was the signal to bring Taylor here."

"Ah, then, it's Taylor," he cried triumphantly. "It's Taylor!"

"Oh, I didn't mean to tell," she said, startled at the admission. "I didn't mean to let anyone know."

"I wish you had told me before," he said with regret, "we could both have been spared some unhappy moments. I know Taylor and his way of fighting, and this thing is going to a finish."

"Go, before he comes," she entreated.

"And leave you alone to face him?" he said more tenderly. "Leave you to a man who fights as he does?" He looked at her for a moment in silence and then bowed his head over her white hand and kissed it. "I can't do that. I love you."

"Oh, please go while there's time," she pleaded; "he mustn't take you." She looked up at him and without shame, revealed the love that she now knew she must ever have for him. "Oh, I couldn't bear that," she said tremulously, "I couldn't."

He gazed down at her, not yet daring to believe that out of this black moment the greatest happiness of his life had come. "Ethel!" he said, amazed.

"I love you," she whispered; "oh, my dear, I love you."

He gathered her in his strong arms. "Then I can fight the whole world," he cried, "and win!"

"For my sake, go," she begged. "Let me see him first; let me try to get you out of it."

"I stay here, dearest," he said firmly. "When he comes, say that you've caught me."

"No, no," she implored; "I can't send you to prison either."

"I'm not going to prison," he reassured her. "I'm not done for yet, but we must save your sister and get that warrant. He must not think you've failed him. Do you understand?"

"But he'll take you away," she cried, and clung to him.

"Do as I say," he besought her; "tell him the necklace is here somewhere. Be brave, my dear, we're working to save your sister. He's coming."

"Hands up, Denby," Taylor shouted, clambering from the balcony to the room and levelling a revolver at the smuggler. Without a word Denby's hands went up as he was bid, and the deputy-surveyor smiled the victor's smile.

"Well, congratulations, Miss Cartwright," he cried; "you landed him as I knew you could if you tried."

"What's the meaning of this?" Denby cried indignantly. "Who are you?"

"Oh, can that bunk!" Taylor said in disgust.

"Where's the necklace, Miss Cartwright?"

"I don't know," she answered nervously.

"You don't know?" he returned incredulously.

"I haven't been able to find it, but it's here somewhere."

"He's probably got it on him," Taylor said.

"All this is preposterous," Denby exclaimed angrily.

"Hand it over," Taylor snapped.

"I have no necklace," Denby told him.

"Then I'll have to search you," he cried, coming to him and going through his pockets with the practised hand of one who knows where to look, covering him the while with the revolver.

"I'll make you pay for this," Denby cried savagely, as Taylor unceremoniously spun him around.

"Will you give it to me," Taylor demanded when he had drawn blank, "or shall I have to upset the place by searching for it?"

"How can I get it for you with my hands up in the air?" Denby asked after a pause. "Let me put my hands down and I'll help you."

Taylor considered for a moment. Few men were better in a rough-and-tumble fight than he, and he had little fear of this beaten man before him. "You haven't got a gun," he said, "so take 'em down, but don't you fool with me."

Denby moved over to the writing-desk and picked up a heavy beaten copper ash-tray with match-box attached. He balanced it in his hand for a moment. "Not a bad idea is it?" he demanded smiling; and then, before Taylor could reach for it had hurled it with the strong arm and practised eye of an athlete straight at the patent burglar alarm a few feet distant.

There was a smashing of glass and then, an instant later, the turning off of light and a plunge into blackness. And in the gloom, during which Taylor thrashed about him wildly, there came from all parts of the house the steady peal of the electrical alarms newly set in motion.

And last of all there was the report of the revolver and a woman's shriek and the falling of a heavy body on the floor, and then a silence.

CHAPTER FOURTEEN

NO sooner had Michael Harrington seated himself at the card-table with his wife and Nora than he picked up a magazine and, as he always said, "kept the light from his eyes." Some men—few there be—who boldly state they desire to sleep, but Michael was of the tactful majority and merely kept the light from his eyes and, incidentally, prevented any observers from noting that his eyes were closed.

He considered this a better way of waiting for Monty than to chatter as the women were doing of the events of the night.

"I wonder what's become of Monty?" Alice asked presently.

"He's kept us twenty minutes," Nora returned crossly. "I saw him go out in the garden. He said it was to relieve his headache, but I really believe he wanted to capture the gang single-handed. Wouldn't it be thrilling if he did?"

"A little improbable," Alice laughed; "but still men do the oddest things sometimes. I never thought Michael the fighting kind till he knocked a man down once for kissing his hand to me."

"It was fine of Michael," Nora said. "The man deserved it."

"I know, dear," her hostess said, "but, as it happens, the man was kissing his hand to his infant son six months old in an upper window. It cost Michael fifty dollars, but I loved him all the more for it. Look at the dear old thing slumbering peacefully and imagining I think he's keeping this very gentle light from his eyes."

"It's the two highballs he had in Mr. Denby's room," the sapient ingénue explained. She harked back to Monty. "I wish he were as brave about proposing. I've tried my grandmother's recipes for shy men, and all my mother ever knew, I know. And yet he does get so flustered when he tries, that he scares himself away."

Alice nodded. "He's the kind you've got to lead to the altar. I had trouble with Michael. He imagined himself too hopelessly old, and very nearly married quite an elderly female. He'd have been dead now if he had. Here's your prey coming in now."

Monty entered the card-room from the garden, nervously stuffing into his pocket the precious package which Denby had thrown to him.

"I hope I haven't delayed the game," he apologized.

"We didn't even miss you," Nora said acidly.

"Were you supposed to be in on this game?"

"Don't be cross, Nora," Alice advised; "you can see his headache has been troubling him. Is it better, Monty?"

"What headache?" he asked. "I haven't had a headache for months. Oh, yes," he added, confused, "that neuralgic headache has gone, thanks. Shall we play?"

"Yes, let's," Nora said. "Michael dealt before he went to sleep."

"Wake up, Michael," his wife said, tapping him with her fan, "you're not at the opera; you're playing cards."

"I haven't slept for a moment," he assured her, after a pause in which he got his bearings. "The light was too strong—"

"So you shaded your eyes," his wife went on. "Well, when they are unshaded will you remember we're playing?"

"Who opened it?" he demanded with a great effort.

"Bridge, my dear," Alice reminded him, "not poker—bridge, auction bridge." She paused a moment while the clock struck three. "And it's three o'clock, and it's quite time you began."

"One no trump," Nora said, after looking at her hand cheerfully.

"It isn't your bid," Alice corrected her, "although I don't wonder you forgot. It's Michael's; he dealt."

Michael tried to concentrate his gaze on his hand. There seemed to be an enormous number of cards, and he needed time to consider the phenomenon.

"What'd the dealer draw?" he asked.

"But we're not playing poker," Alice said.

"It was Monty who confused me," he said in excuse, and looked reproachfully at his vis-à-vis. "What's trumps?"

"It's your bid," Nora cried. "You dealt."

"I go one spade."

"One no trump," Monty declared.

"Two royals," Nora cried, not that she had them, but to take it away from Monty.

"Pass," said Alice glumly. She could have gone two royals, but dared not risk three.

"Give me three cards," Michael cried more cheerfully. The way was becoming clearer.

"Michael," his wife said reprovingly, "if you're really as tired as that, you'd better go to bed."

"I never broke up a poker game in my life," he cried. "It's only the shank of the evening. What's happened, partner?" he yawned to Nora.

"I went two royals," she said.

Michael looked at his hand enthusiastically. "Three aces," he murmured. "I'd like to open it for two dollars—as it is, I pass."

"Two no trumps," said Monty. When the rest had passed, Nora led and Monty played from the dummy. Michael, at last feeling he was rounding into form, played a low card, so that dummy took the trick with a nine.

"Anything wrong?" he asked anxiously as Nora shook her head.

"If you don't want to win you're playing like a bridge article in a Sunday paper," she returned.

"This game makes me sick," he said in disgust. "Nothing but reproaches."

"I wish Mr. Denby were playing instead of poor Michael," Nora remarked.

"Steve's got the right idea," Monty commented. "He's in bed."

"Great man, Denby," said Michael. "He knows you can't sit up all night unless you drink."

"We'll finish the rubber and then stop," his wife said comfortingly. "Do remember it's not poker."

"I wish it were," he exclaimed dolefully. "No partners—no reproaches—no post-mortems in poker. If you make a fool of yourself you lose your own money and everybody else is glad of it and gets cheerful."

"After this then, one round of jacks to please Michael," said Alice.

"And then quit," Monty suggested. "I'm tired, too."

"I'm not tired," Michael asserted. "I'm only thirsty. It takes this form with me. When I'm thirsty—"

Michael stopped in consternation. Overhead, from all parts of the house, came the mechanical announcement that burglars had broken in. The four rose simultaneously from the table.

"Burglars!" cried Michael, looking from one to the other.

"Good Heavens!" Nora gasped.

"What shall we do?" cried Alice.

"It's gone off by accident," Monty asserted quivering, as there came suddenly the sound of a shot.

"Somebody's killed!" Alice exclaimed, with an air of certainty.

Michael was the first to recover his poise. "Monty," he commanded sternly, "go and find what's the matter. I'll look after the girls."

Alice looked at him entreatingly. "You'd better go," she said; "I shall feel safer if you see what it is. You're not afraid, Michael?"

"Certainly not," he said with dignity. "Of course they're armed. Hello, who's here?"

It was Lambart entering, bearing in his hand a .45 revolver.

"The burglar-alarm, sir," he said, with as little excitement as he might have announced the readiness of dinner. "The indicator points to Mr. Denby's room."

"Good old Lambart," his employer said heartily. "You go ahead, and we'll follow. No, you keep the beastly thing," he exclaimed, when the butler handed him the weapon. "You're a better shot than I am, Lambart."

"Mikey," Alice called to him, "if you're going to be killed, I want to be killed, too."

The Harringtons followed the admirable Lambart up the stairway, while Nora gazed after them with a species of fascinated curiosity that was not compounded wholly of fear. Intensely alive to the vivid interest of these swiftly moving scenes through which she was passing, Nora—although she could scream with the best of them—was not in reality badly scared.

"I don't want to be killed," she announced with decision.

Monty moved to her side. He had an idea that if he must die or be arrested, he would like Nora to live on, cherishing the memory that he was a man.

"Neither do I!" he cried. "I wish I'd never gone into this. I knew when I dreamed about Sing Sing last night that it meant something."

"Gone into what?" Nora demanded.

"I'm liable to get shot any minute."

"What!" she cried anxiously.

"This may be my last five minutes on earth, Nora."

"Oh, Monty," she returned, "what have you done?" She looked at him in ecstatic admiration; never had he seemed so heroic and desirable. "Was it murder?"

"If I come out of it alive, will you marry me?" he asked desperately.

"Oh, Monty!" she exclaimed, and flung herself into his arms. "Why did you put it off so long?"

"I didn't need your protection so much," he told her; "and anyway it takes a crisis like this to make me say what I really feel."

"I love you anyway, no matter what you've done," she said contentedly.

He looked at her more brightly. "I'm the happiest man in the world," he declared, "providing," he added cautiously, "I don't get shot."

She raised her head from his shoulder and tapped the package in his pocket. "What's that?" she asked.

"That's my heart," he said sentimentally.

"But why do you wear it on the right side?" she queried.

"Oh, that," he said more gravely, "I'd forgotten all about it. It belongs to Steve. That shows I love you," he added firmly; "I'd forgotten all about it."

As he spoke there was the shrill call of a police whistle outside. "The police!" he gasped.

"Don't let them get you," she whispered. "They are coming this way."

"Quick," he said, grabbing her arm and leading her to a door. "We'll hide here." Now that danger, as he apprehended it, was definitely at hand, his spirits began to rise. He was of the kind which finds in suspense the greatest horror. They had barely reached the shelter of a door when Duncan and Gibbs ran in.

"Come on, Harry," Duncan called to the slower man, "he's upstairs. Get your gun ready."

Nora clasped her lover's hand tighter. "There'll be some real shooting," she whispered; "I hope Alice doesn't get hurt. Listen!"

"The Chief's got him for sure," Gibbs panted, making his ascent at the best speed he could gather.

"They've gone," Nora said, peering out; then she ventured into the hall. "Who's the chief?" she asked.

"The chief of police I guess," he groaned. "This is awful, Nora. I can't have you staying here with all this going on. Go back into the card-room, and I'll let you know what's happened as soon as I can."

"But what are you going to do?" she asked.

"I'm going to wait for Steve; he's very likely to want me."

"I'm not afraid," Nora said airily.

"But I am," he retorted; "I'm afraid for you. Be a good girl and do as I say, and I'll come as soon as the trouble's over."

"I just hate to miss anything," she pouted. "Still if you really wish it." She looked at him more tenderly than he had ever seen her look at any human being before. "Don't get killed, Monty, dear."

Monty took her in his arms and kissed her. "I don't want to," he said, "especially now."

When the door had shut behind her he took out the necklace with the idea of secreting it in an unfindable place. He remembered a Poe story where a letter was hidden in so obvious a spot that it defied Parisian commissaries of police. But the letters were usual things and pearl necklaces were not, and he took it down from the mantel where for a second he had let it lie, and rammed it under a sofa-cushion on the nearby couch. That, too, was not a brilliant idea and, while he was wondering if the pearls would dissolve if he dropped them in a decanter of whiskey on a table near him, there were loud voices heard at the head of the stairway, and he fled from the spot.

CHAPTER FIFTEEN

WHEN the Harringtons followed their butler into Denby's room, they were appalled at what they could not see but heard without difficulty. A strange voice, a harsh, coarse voice rapping out oaths and imprecations, a man fighting with some opponent who remained silent. While they who owned the house stood helpless, Lambart turned on the lights.

The sudden glare showed them Denby was the silent fighter. The other man, a heavily built fellow, seemed for the moment blinded by the lights, and stopped for a second. And it was in this second that Denby uppercut him so that he fell with a thud to the floor.

Then they saw Denby pick up a revolver that was lying by the stranger's side.

"What's the matter?" cried Michael, while Lambart busied himself with making the room tidy and replacing overturned chairs.

"This man," said Denby, still panting from his efforts, "tried to break in, and Miss Cartwright and I got him."

"Good Lord!" Michael ejaculated.

"How splendid of you!" Alice cried. "Ethel, you're a heroine, my dear."

Taylor, who had not been put out by the blow, scrambled to his feet and was pushed into a chair. Denby stood conveniently near with the revolver a foot from his heart.

"I never saw a more typical criminal," Michael said, severely looking at the captive; "every earmark of it. I could pick him out of a thousand. Now, Denby, we want to hear all about it."

"He's crazy," Taylor shouted indignantly. "Don't you believe him. He's the crook. I'm an agent of the United States Customs and I came here to get Denby."

"That's a pretty poor bluff," Denby scoffed. "This porch climber was one of the two who held up Monty and Miss Rutledge in the grounds to-night."

"I said they'd break in!" Alice cried, and believed her statement. "And how fortunate Ethel moved her room. This man looks like the sort who wouldn't stop short of murder, Michael."

"The lowest human type!" Michael cried. "Look at his eyes and ears, and nose!"

"I tell you I came to arrest him!" Taylor cried, striving to keep his already ruffled temper.

"Arrest that charming man?" Mrs. Harrington cried with scorn. "Was there ever anything so utterly absurd!"

"Absurd!" he sneered. "You won't think so when you learn who I am. Ask that girl there; she knows; she'll tell you whether I'm absurd."

Instantly they all centred their gaze on Ethel. For a second she looked at him blankly. "I never saw the man before," she told them.

"You didn't, eh?" Taylor cried, after a pause of sheer astonishment, "I guess you'll remember me when I serve a warrant for your sister's arrest. It's in my pocket now with other papers that prove I'm working for the United States Government." He made a motion as though to get them but found Denby's gun close under his nose.

"No you don't," Denby warned him. "You've probably got a neat little automatic pistol there. I know your sort."

But when he seemed about to relieve the deputy-collector of his papers Taylor shouted a loud protest.

"Very well," Denby cried. "If you had rather Mr. Harrington did, it's all the same to me. Mr. Harrington," turning to his host, "will you please remove whatever documents you find in his inner pocket, so that we may find out if what he says is true."

"Surely," Michael returned. "I like every man to have justice even if the electric chair yearns for him." Carefully he removed a bundle of papers neatly tied together. And one of them, as Ethel Cartwright saw, was the warrant made out for her sister's arrest. She wondered why Denby had invited inspection of them, but was not long to remain in doubt.

"Now," said Michael judicially, "we'll do the thing properly."

But before he had unfolded a single one of the papers, they were snatched violently from his hand, and Denby, gun pointed at Taylor, was backing to the door. "Keep out of range, Harrington," the retreating man warned. He cast a swift look of triumph toward Ethel. "It's all right, Miss Cartwright," he called cheerfully. "Don't worry, it's all right now."

As the door closed, Taylor sprang from the chair with a curse. "Grab him, I tell you," he cried raging. "He's a crook. The Government wants him, and they'll hold you people responsible if he gets away." He blew his whistle loudly, and then rushed out of the door and down the hall taking the steps four at a time.

The French windows were open and out of them he ran, calling sharply for his men. But Gibbs and Duncan were even now fiercely searching the other wing and disturbing frightened servants above. It was not for some minutes that they made their way to their chief, and searched the grounds as he bade them.

And even here they were frustrated. Lambart's tactical genius had forbidden him to remove the clothes-lines he had laid to bring wandering tramps low, and among them Duncan and Gibbs floundered with dreadful profanity.

There were two other men aiding them now, Ford and Hammett, who were stationed outside the grounds to watch the only road by which Denby could escape. When Taylor was satisfied they were doing what they could, he came back into the big hall where the frightened group was awaiting him.

"We'll get your friend yet," he observed disagreeably to Mrs. Harrington. "It's bright moonlight, and my men'll nab him."

"But he's not my friend," she objected; "I had no idea he was that kind of a person."

"When I find a man like that a guest in a house like this," Taylor retorted, "I think I'm justified in calling him your friend. You'll have time to think what to say later when you're called as a witness."

"I want to beg your pardon, Mr. Taylor," said Michael anxiously. The idea of being cross-examined and made a fool of by a bullying counsel horrified him. He'd be a jest forever more at Meadow Brook and Piping Rock. The Harringtons casually to pick up a smuggler and make him free of their exclusive home! Never had he needed a drink to steady his nerves as he did now!

"Well, I certainly think there is an apology due me," Taylor sneered. He was not one to forget an affront and Harrington had alluded to his criminal type in a way that rankled yet.

"But how could we know?" asked Mrs. Harrington; "he seemed perfectly all right, although I did say he might be a murderer."

"That'll come out in court," Taylor reminded her disagreeably. "If it hadn't been that my men were here to swear to me, I'd have spent the night in one of your little one-horse jails, and he'd have got away. When I do get him he'll remember Daniel Taylor till the day he dies."

Monty, overhearing these direful threats from behind a door, and happy because of his friend's escape, walked boldly in.

"Did you get the burglar?" he demanded airily.

"There wasn't any burglar," Alice told him.

"It was your old friend Denby that caused all the trouble," Michael informed him, "the old friend you introduced into my house. I tell you, Monty—"

"Don't explain," Taylor commanded. "Now," he snapped to Monty, "have you seen Steven Denby in the last ten minutes?"

Monty found with glee that so far from being nervous he was enjoying the scene. He only regretted that his moustache was not long enough to permit him to curl it to a fierce and martial angle. He was glad that Nora had crept into the room and was watching him.

"Isn't he in bed?" he demanded, yawning.

"You know he isn't in bed," Taylor answered. "Maybe you're his pal—in on this job with him. Come here."

Monty wished to refuse, but Taylor had a compelling manner, so he advanced with an insolent slowness.

Alice Harrington flew to his defence. "That's too absurd!" she cried. "We've known Mr. Vaughan since he was a child."

"Who is this person?" Monty demanded superciliously.

"Never mind who I am," Taylor said gruffly, and started to search him.

"Don't hurt him," Nora cried, rushing to her fiancé's side.

"It's all right, Nora," Monty said; submitting quietly. "He thinks he's doing his duty. When you're through with me," he said to Taylor, "I'll take you to my room. You'd probably like to go through that, too."

"Here, that'll be enough from you," Taylor said frowning. "You aren't smart enough to be Denby's pal. Clear out—get back to the nursery."

Nora cast a glance of vivid hatred at him, but Taylor turned his back on her.

"Do you want us any longer?" Michael asked.

"No," he was told. "You can go and leave me with this girl," pointing to Ethel, who had not said a word. "I want a little talk with her."

"Please keep her out of it," Michael asked him. "I'm sure she's absolutely innocent in the matter."

Taylor looked at him, exasperated. "See here," he cried, "you've put enough obstacles in my way to-night as it is! Do you want to put any more?"

"It's all right," Ethel Cartwright said quickly; "there's just some misunderstanding. Please go!"

"All right, then," her host answered. "Come, Alice, I need a drink badly."

"My dear," she said affectionately, "under the circumstances you may have an all-night license."

He had turned to go when Lambart approached him. "I beg your pardon, sir, but can I have a word with you?" "What is it?" Michael demanded anxiously. The news evidently affected him, and Taylor looked suspicious. "What's this mean?" the deputy-surveyor asked.

"A long distance from my partner," the agitated Harrington returned. "I stand to lose nearly a million dollars if something isn't done. Excuse me, Alice—I'll use the upstairs 'phone." He hurried upstairs.

"Well," said Monty to Taylor—Nora was hanging on his arm and he felt he would never again be afraid—"do you want me any longer?"

"I thought I sent you back to play," Taylor snarled.

Ostentatiously Monty turned his back and walked leisurely to a door.

"You are perfectly splendid," Nora exclaimed with ecstasy in her voice. "I'd no idea you were so brave."

"Oh, you can never tell," Monty returned modestly.

Alice joined them in retreat. "Michael's thirst is catching," she asserted. "I'm for some champagne, children, are you?"

"Sure," said Monty. "What's a quart amongst three?"

Taylor watched them depart, sneeringly. He hated the idle rich with the intensity of a man who has longed to be of them and knows he cannot. The look he flung at Miss Cartwright was not pleasant.

"What did you mean by telling them upstairs that you had never seen me before?" he cried vindictively.

"You said under no circumstances was I to mention your name."

He looked a trifle disconcerted at this simple explanation. He was in a mood for punishment, and rebuke.

"Yes," he admitted, "but—"

"You said it was imperative your identity should not be disclosed," the girl reminded him.

"I suppose that's true in a way," he conceded; "but when you saw me wanting to prove who I was, why didn't you help?"

"I was afraid to do anything but follow your instructions," she said earnestly. "I remembered that you swore you'd put my sister in prison if I even said I'd ever seen you before."

"Well, then, we won't say any more about it," he returned ungraciously. "How did you find Denby had the necklace?"

"I got into his room and caught him," she explained. "He had it in his hand."

"Yes, yes!" he cried impatiently; "go on."

"And when the lights went out and there was a shot, I screamed, and naturally I couldn't see what happened in the dark. I thought you had killed him and I was frightened."

Taylor frowned. He did not like to remember that directly the flash of his gun had disclosed his position Denby had sprung on him like an arrow and knocked him down. Denby had scored two knock-downs in one night, and none had ever done that before. There was a swelling on his jaw and three teeth were loosened. Denby should pay for that, he swore.

While he was thinking these vengeful thoughts, Duncan hurried in through the French windows.

"Say, Chief," he shouted, "Denby didn't leave the house. He's up in his room now."

"How do you know?" Taylor cried eagerly.

"Gibbs climbed up on the roof of the pagoda; he can see the room from there and Denby's in it now."

"Now we've got him sure," his chief cried gleefully.

"And Harrington's with him," Duncan added excitedly.

"What!" Taylor ejaculated, stopping short on his way to the stairs. The two men talking together spelled collusion to him, and opened up complications to which he had hardly given a thought.

"Gibbs said they were talking together," his subordinate continued.

"I was right at first," Taylor exclaimed; "I thought that might be the game, but he fooled me so that I would have sworn he was innocent. Denby's smuggling the necklace through for Harrington. Jim, this is a big job, get out there to make sure he don't escape by the balcony. Have your gun handy," he warned; "I've got mine." He looked over to Ethel, whose face betrayed the anguish which she was enduring. "And I'll get the drop on him this time."

"No, no," she cried, "you mustn't!"

"You knew all the time he was back in his room and you've been trying to fool me—you're stuck on him."

"No, no, you're wrong," she said desperately.

"Am I?" he retorted; "then I'll give you the chance to prove it. Send for Denby and ask him what he did with the necklace, and where it is now. Tell him I suspect you, and that he's got to tell you the truth, but you won't turn him over to me. Talk as if you two were alone, but I'll be there behind that screen listening." He took out his revolver and pointed to it meaningly. "If you tip him off or give him the slightest warning or signal, I'll arrest you both, anyway. Wrong, am I?" he sneered. "We'll see; and if you try to fool me again, you and your sister will have plenty of time to think it over in Auburn. Now send for him."

There was a big screen of tapestry in one corner of the hall near the stairs. Behind this he had little difficulty in hiding himself.

The girl watched him in terror. It seemed she must either offer the man she loved bound and helpless to his enemies, or else by warning him and aiding him in escape, see him shot before her eyes. There seemed here no way out with Taylor watching her every look and movement from his hiding-place.

She stretched out her tremulous hand to grasp the table for support and clutched instead the silver cigarette-box, the same she had offered earlier to Denby. Her deep dejection was banished for she saw here a chance to defeat her enemy by a ruse of which he could not know. Watching her, Taylor saw her returning courage, and congratulated her. She knew, he thought, that her only chance was to play the square game with him now.

"Well," he called from his concealment, "why don't you send for him?"

"I'm going to!" she answered, walking to the bell and then coming back to the table. "You'll see you've been all wrong about me."

"I guess not," he snarled, adjusting the screen so as better to be able to see her from between its folds. He noticed that Lambart passing close to him as he answered the bell had no suspicion of his presence.

"Mr. Denby's in his room," she told the man, "please say I'm alone here and wish to speak to him at once."

"Yes, madam," Lambart said, and a few seconds later could be heard knocking at a distant door.

"I can see you perfectly," Taylor warned her. "When Denby comes in, stay right where you are and don't move, or else I'll—" He stopped short when Lambart descended the staircase.

"Mr. Denby will be with you immediately," the butler said, and left the hall.

CHAPTER SIXTEEN

DENBY came eagerly down the stairs, looking about him with no especial care. He had learned that the special service men assumed him to have made good his escape and were contenting themselves with surrounding the gardens.

"What's happened?" he asked, coming quickly toward her. "Is everything all right now? Where is—"

Ethel interrupted him. "Will you have a cigarette, Dick?" she asked, pushing the silver box to him.

He took it calmly enough but instantly realized her warning. His alert gaze swept about the room and dwelt no longer on the screen than any other of its furnishing, but he knew where his enemy was hidden. "Thanks," he said simply, and lighted it with a hand that was steady.

"Now we are alone," she said, "and those men imagine you are not here, and I admit you've beaten me, please tell me the truth about that necklace. What have you done with it?"

"Are you still persisting in that strange delusion?" he asked calmly. "I never had a necklace, Miss Cartwright."

"But I know you did," she persisted, "I saw it."

"Ah, you thought you did," he corrected. "We went all over that in my room and I imagined I had persuaded you. Why do you want to know this?"

"The agent of the secret service has been here," she told him, "and he suspects that I am defending you and won't believe what I say. If you'll tell me the truth, I'll get him to let you go."

"Then the secret service agent is just as wrong as you," he remarked. "I have no necklace. Because I knock down a man who breaks into my room at night and escape rather than be shot, am I supposed on that account to carry these fabulous necklaces about with me? I don't care even to prolong this conversation, Miss Cartwright."

At this point Lambart entered, and coming toward him, delivered a small package.

"Pardon me, sir," the butler began, "but Mr Vaughan asked me to take this to your room."

"What is it?" Denby asked, and a slight movement behind the screen betokened the curiosity of the man hidden there.

"Mr. Vaughan didn't say, sir," Lambart returned. "He only said it was very important for you to get it immediately." Lambart bowed and retired.

"I wonder what on earth Monty can be sending me at this time of the night," said Denby, balancing the thing as though to judge its contents from the weight. "It must be important, so forgive me if I see what it is."

He tore the envelope open carelessly, and out of it dropped the necklace. Quickly he stooped down and picked it up, putting it in his left-hand coat-pocket.

The girl could not refrain from giving a cry as he did so. "Oh," she exclaimed, "we're done for now."

There was a crash behind them as the screen clattered to the floor and Daniel Taylor stepped over it, levelled gun in hand.

"Hands up, Denby," he commanded, and then blew his police whistle.

He looked sourly at the trembling girl by the table. "I don't know how you tipped him off, but you two are damned smart, aren't you? But I've got you both now, so it's just as well it happened as it did."

Gibbs and Duncan burst in, their anxious faces breaking into smiles of joy. The Chief's temper if his plans miscarried was a fixed quantity and an unpleasant one. They had been consoling themselves outside, and Duncan had been wishing he had Gibbs' outside job. Now everything would be well and they would each be able to boast in his home circle of to-night's exploit.

"You're both under arrest," Taylor said, addressing his captives. "Boys," he commanded his satellites cordially, "take her into one of those side rooms and keep her there till I call. They can talk without speaking, these two. I'll question 'em separately."

For the second time within an hour he searched Denby. From the right-hand pocket of his dinner jacket he took an automatic pistol. From the left he drew out the string of pearls.

"It's a pippin, all right," Taylor muttered, his eyes gloating over the treasure. "How much did you pay the girl?"

"Not a cent," his prisoner asserted. "Nothing. You're all wrong there."

"Then why did she tip you off just now?"

"She didn't tip me off," Denby told him. "She didn't say a word, as you yourself must have heard."

"Can it! can it!" Taylor retorted impatiently. "I saw the result all right, but I couldn't get on to the cause. What did she do it for?"

Denby shrugged his shoulders and smiled a little. It was the first time he had come off his high horse.

"Maybe," he hinted, "she didn't want to see me go to prison."

"Oh, you pulled the soft stuff, eh?" Taylor said. "Well, she tried to double-cross me and that don't pay, Denby. She'll find that out, all right."

Denby assumed a certain confidential air. "Look here, Taylor," he said, "so long as she did the decent thing by me, I'd like to see her out of this. You've got me, and you've got the pearls—Why not let her go?"

Taylor shook his head. He did not signalize his triumphs by the freeing of captives or the giving of rewards. "I guess not," he returned with his sourest look. "You've both given me a lot of unnecessary trouble, and I think a little trip down south ought to fix you two comfortably. What do you say to five years in Atlanta? Fine winter climate they say."

"Then I guess we are up against it;" Denby sighed.

"You are, son," Taylor assured him; "right up against it."

"Take it out on me," the other implored; "ease up on her. It isn't as if she were a grafter, either. Why, I offered her twenty thousand dollars to square it."

"Tried to bribe a Government official, eh?" Taylor observed. "That don't make it any better for you."

"Oh, you can't prove it against me," Denby returned easily.

"Twenty thousand dollars," Taylor muttered; "twenty thousand dollars! So you *were* trying to smuggle it in for the Harringtons, then?"

"I hate bringing names in," said Denby, looking at him shrewdly.

"Well, they'll have to come out in court anyway," the other reminded him, and then reverted to the money. "Twenty thousand dollars!" he repeated. "It seems to mean a whole lot to you—or somebody—to get this through, eh?"

"It does," Denby returned, "and it's a big lot of money; but I'd rather pay that than sample your winter climate down south—see?" He looked at him still with that air of confidence as though he expected Taylor to comprehend his motives.

"Say, what are you trying to do?" Taylor said sharply; "bribe me?"

"What an imagination you have!" Denby said in astonishment. "Why, you couldn't be bribed, Mr. Taylor!"

"You bet your life I couldn't," the deputy-surveyor returned.

Denby sighed. "What a pity I didn't meet a business man instead of *you*."

Taylor's sharp eyes looked at the speaker steadily.

"You couldn't square it even with a business man for twenty thousand dollars."

Denby met his shrewd gaze without lowering his eyes.

"If I'd met the right kind of business man," he declared, "I shouldn't have offered twenty thousand dollars," he said meaningly; "I'd have offered him all I've got—and that's thirty thousand dollars."

A slow smile chased Taylor's intent expression away. "You would?" he said.

"I would," Denby answered steadily.

"A business man," Taylor returned, "wouldn't believe you had that much unless he saw it with his own eyes."

"I should prove it," Denby answered. And with his first and second finger he probed behind his collar and produced three new ten-thousand-dollar bills.

"Beauties, aren't they?" he asked of the staring Taylor.

The official seemed hypnotized by them. "I didn't know they made 'em that big," he said reverently.

When Denby next spoke, his tone was brisker. "Look here, Taylor, I haven't been in Paris for two years."

There was understanding in Taylor's face now. "You haven't?" he returned.

"And in case of a come-back, I've witnesses to prove an alibi."

"You have?" Taylor responded, his smile broadening.

"How much does the Government pay you?" Denby questioned.

Taylor's eyes were still on the bills. "Three thousand a year," he answered.

Denby inspected the crisp bills interestedly. "Ten years' salary!" he commented. "You couldn't save all this honestly in your lifetime."

Denby raised his eyes and the two men looked at one another and a bargain was as certainly made as though documents had been drawn up attesting it.

Taylor's manner altered instantly. He removed his hat and became a genial, not to say jocular, soul.

"Too bad," he said sympathetically, "a mistake like that happening."

"It is a bit inconvenient," Denby allowed.

"I'm sorry to have bothered you," the deputy-surveyor assured him, "but you're all right, Mr. Denby. I figured from the first that you might be a business man, and that's why you slipped through so easily."

"You're a pretty smart man, Mr. Taylor," Denby admitted, "and I think these belong to you." He held out the money.

"Yes, I think they do," Taylor said eagerly, reaching out for the bills.

"Wait a minute!" Denby cried, holding the money back. "How do I know you won't take it and then double-cross me?"

"I'll give you my word for it," Taylor assured him fervently.

"That security isn't good enough," Denby remarked slowly. "We haven't done business together before, and those two men of yours—are they in on it?"

"Not on your life," Taylor laughed. "I haven't split with anybody for five years. This is a one man job, Mr. Denby."

"That may be," the other protested, "but they saw you pinch me!"

"I'll tell them it was all a mistake and I've got to call it off. I know the kind of help I want when I'm tackling a one man job."

"Do you think you can get away with it?" Denby asked doubtfully.

"I always have," Taylor said simply. "There's no need for you to get scared."

Denby still seemed perturbed. "I've been hearing a lot about this R. J.," he told the official. "I don't like what I've heard either. Is he suspicious about you by any chance?"

"What do you know about R. J.?" Taylor asked quickly.

"Some friends of mine—business men—in London, tipped me off about him. They said he's been investigating the bribery rumors in the Customs."

"Don't you worry about him, my boy," Taylor said with a reassuring air, "I'm the guy on this job."

"That's all well enough," Denby said, "but I don't want to give up thirty thousand and then get pinched as well. I've got to think about myself."

Taylor leaned across eagerly. "Say, if that R. J. has scared you into thinking he'll ball things up, I don't mind admitting—in strict confidence—who he is."

"So you know?" Denby retorted. "Who is he? I want to be on my guard."

"Well, he isn't a thousand miles from here."

"What!" Denby cried in astonishment.

Taylor tapped himself upon the chest with an air of importance. "Get me?"

"Well, that's funny," Denby laughed.

"What's funny?" Taylor retorted.

"Why, R. J. is supposed to be death on grafters and you're one yourself."

"I'm a business man," Taylor said with a wink. "I'm not a grafter—I should worry about the Government."

"Well I guess I'll take a chance," Denby said, after a momentary pause.

"That's the idea," Taylor cried cheerfully.

"Provided," Denby added, "you let me have a few words with your men. They've got to understand I'm innocent, and I want to see how they take it. You see, I don't know them as well as you do. They've got to back you up in squaring me with the Harringtons. You've put me in all wrong here, remember."

"Why sure," Taylor agreed generously, "talk your head off to 'em."

"And you'll leave the girl out of it?"

"I'll do more than that," Taylor told him with a grin; "I'll leave her to you."

Denby heaved a sigh of relief. "Now we understand one another," he said. "Here's your money, Taylor."

"Much obliged," Taylor responded. He handed the other the pearls. "I've no evidence," he declared in high good humor, "that you ever had any necklace. Have a cigar, Mr. Denby?"

**"NOW WE UNDERSTAND ONE ANOTHER," HE SAID.
"HERE'S YOUR MONEY."**

"Thanks," the younger man returned; "I'll smoke it later it you don't mind. Now call 'em in."

"Certainly," Taylor said briskly. "And say, I'm glad to have met you, Mr. Denby; and next time you're landing in New York and I can be of use, let me know." He leered. "I might be of considerable use, understand?"

CHAPTER SEVENTEEN

TAYLOR walked briskly across the hall and threw open the door of the room in which his subordinates were guarding their prisoner. "Duncan," he called, "and Gibbs, come here."

When they had come in with Ethel Cartwright, he turned to them impressively. "Boys," he declared, "it was all a mistake."

"What!" cried his men.

"Thank God!" the girl cried softly.

"Our dope was phoney. We were tipped off wrong by someone, out of mischief or malice—I'll have to look into that—and we're all in wrong. It was a case of mistaken identity, but Mr. Denby's been very nice about it, very nice, indeed. Let the lady go, Jim."

"I asked Mr. Taylor to send for you," Denby explained, "because I thought it was due you, and I didn't want any come-back. I want you all to understand the facts, if you don't mind waiting, Miss Cartwright."

"Of course I'll wait," she said brightly. What had happened to change things she could not guess, but she was confident the man she loved had some magic to save them both.

"Listen to him, boys," Taylor counselled. "You see, he's a bit anxious to straighten things out, so tell him all you know. Fire ahead, Mr. Denby."

Denby addressed himself to James Duncan. "You got a tip from Harlow that a Steven Denby had bought a necklace at Cartier's?"

"Yes, sir," Duncan agreed.

Denby now turned to Gibbs who assumed a character of importance.

"Then you got a wireless that this Denby had sailed with Mrs. Michael Harrington and Mr. Montague Vaughan, which threw suspicion on the lady as a possible smuggler?"

"That's right, too," Gibbs conceded, contentedly.

"And yet," Denby remarked with inquiry in his tone, "you let Denby slip through the Customs to-day, didn't you?"

Taylor's satisfied expression had faded partially. "You see," he explained, "we didn't have any absolute evidence to arrest him on."

"Just what I was going to say," Gibbs remarked.

"But after he got through," Denby went on, "you received an anonymous telegram late this afternoon that Denby carried the necklace in a tobacco-pouch, didn't you?"

Taylor advanced a step frowning. "What's all this, anyway?" he demanded. "How do you know about that telegram?"

"I found it out to-night," Denby said pleasantly.

"That's a private Government matter," Taylor blustered.

Denby looked at him in surprise. "Surely," he said, "you don't object to my making things clear? I was pretty nice to you, Mr. Taylor."

Taylor's fingers nestled tenderly about the crackling notes in his pocket. "All right," he assented, "go ahead."

Denby turned on the expectant Gibbs.

"You knew about that tip in the telegram?"

"First I ever heard about it," Gibbs returned, open-eyed.

"Then you didn't tell them?" Denby observed, looking toward their chief.

"That was my own business," Taylor said impatiently. He wished this fool cross-examination over, and himself out of Long Island.

"Did it ever occur to you boys that it was rather peculiar that this supposed smuggler wasn't searched—that he got through without the slightest trouble?"

"Why, the Chief didn't want to get in any mix-up with the Harringtons in case he was wrong about Denby," Gibbs elucidated.

"Oh, I see," Denby remarked, as though the whole thing were now perfectly straightforward. "He told you that, did he?"

"He sure did," Duncan agreed readily.

"Don't you boys see," Denby said seriously, "that this whole job looks very much as if the scheme was to let Denby slip through and then blackmail him?"

"I never thought of that," Duncan returned.

"Me, neither," the ingenuous Gibbs added.

"Wait a minute," Taylor said irritably. "What's all this got to do with you? I admit we made a mistake—I'll take the blame for it—and we're sorry. We can't remedy it by talking any more. Come on, boys."

"Wait just a minute," Denby exclaimed. "Don't you know," he went on, addressing himself to the two subordinate officials, "that it's rather a dangerous thing to monkey with the United States Government? It's a pretty big thing to fool with. You might have got into serious trouble arresting the wrong man."

"I haven't been monkeying with the Government," Gibbs said nervously. All his official carelessness recurred to him vividly. "I wouldn't do a thing like that."

"Neither have I," Duncan made eager reply.

Taylor took a hand in the conversation. "That's all settled," he said, with an air of finality. "We all know Mr. Denby never had a necklace."

"That's clearly understood, is it?" Denby returned.

"What I say is right," Taylor retorted, and glared at his underlings.

"What the Chief says is right," Gibbs admitted with eagerness.

"What the Chief says is wrong," Denby cried in a different voice. "I did smuggle a necklace in through the Customs to-day. Here it is."

They looked at it in consternation. "What!" they ejaculated.

Taylor had owed his safety ere this to rapid thinking.

"Then you're under arrest!" he cried.

"Oh, no I'm not," Denby rejoined, turning to the startled men. "Your chief caught me with the goods and I paid him thirty thousand dollars to square it."

Taylor came at him with upraised fist. "Why, you—" he roared, "I'll—"

Denby seized the clenched fist and thrust it aside. "You won't," he said calmly; "you're only a bully after all, Taylor. You couldn't graft on your own—you had to drag a girl into it, and you've made me do some pretty rotten things to-night to land you. I've had to make that girl suffer, but you'll pay for it. I've got you now, and you're under arrest."

"Aw, quit your bluffing," Taylor jeered; "you can't arrest me, Denby."

"The man who'll arrest you is named Jones," Denby remarked.

"Who the hell is he?" Taylor cried.

"Ah, yes," Denby admitted. "I forgot that you hadn't met him officially and that the boys don't know who he is either. Here's my commission." Gibbs stared at the document ravenously. "And that's my photograph," Denby added. "A pretty good likeness it's usually considered."

Duncan was now at his comrade's side, poring over it. "It sure is," he agreed.

"This thing," said Gibbs the discoverer, "is made out in the name of Richard Jones!"

"Well, do you get the initials?" Denby queried.

"R. J.," Gibbs read out as one might mystic things without meaning.

"That's me," Denby smiled, "R. J. of the secret service. That's the name I'm known by."

Gibbs offered his hand. "If you're R. J.," he said admiringly, "I'd like to shake hands with you. Are you, on the level, R. J.?"

"I'm afraid I am," the other admitted.

"It's a lie," Taylor shouted.

Denby pointed to the paper. "You can't get away from that signature. It's signed by the President of the United States."

"I tell you it's a fake," the man cried angrily.

"They don't seem to think so," Denby remarked equably.

"This is on the level, all right," Duncan announced after prolonged scrutiny.

Denby turned to the deputy-surveyor.

"Taylor," he said gravely, "for three years the Government has been trying to land the big blackmailer in the Customs. They brought me into it and I set a trap with a necklace as a bait. The whole thing was a plant from Harlow's tip, the telegram I sent myself this afternoon, to the accidental dropping of the pearls, so that you could see them through the screen. You walked right into it, Taylor. Twice before you came and looked into other traps and had some sort of intuition and kept out of them. This time, Taylor, it worked."

"You can't get away with that," Taylor said threateningly. "I'm not going to listen to this."

"Wait a minute," Denby advised him. "You've been in the service long enough to know that the rough stuff won't go. You'd only get the worst of it; so take things easily."

He smiled pleasantly at the other men. "I'm glad to find you boys weren't in on this. Take him along with you, and this, too." He tossed the necklace on the table from which it slid to the floor at Gibbs' feet.

Gibbs made a quick step forward to recover it, but trod on part of the string and crushed many of the stones. Poor Gibbs looked at the damage he had done aghast. If the thing were worth two hundred thousand dollars, a ponderous calculation forced the dreadful knowledge upon him that he had destroyed possibly a quarter of them. Fifty thousand dollars! Tears came to his eyes. "Honest to goodness," he groaned, looking imploringly at the august R. J., "I couldn't help it."

"Don't worry," Denby laughed. "They're fakes. Take what's left as Exhibit A."

Gibbs recovered his ease of manner quickly and took a few steps nearer the fallen Chief. "And to think I've been working for a crook two years and never knew it," he said, with a childlike air of wonder.

Taylor looked at Denby with rage and despair.

"Damn you," he exploded, "you've got me all right, but I'll send that girl and her sister up the river. You're stuck on her and I'll get even that way."

Even in his fury he remarked that this threat did not disturb the man in the least. He saw the girl blanch and hide her face, but this cursed meddling R. J., as he called himself, only smiled.

"I think not," Denby returned. "You forget that Mr. Harrington is vice-president of the New York Burglar Insurance Company and a friend of the late Mr. Vernon Cartwright. I hardly think he will allow a little matter like that to come into public notice. In fact, I've seen him about it already."

"Oh, get me out of this," Taylor cried in disgust.

"Just a minute," Denby commanded. "I'll trouble you for that thirty thousand dollars."

"You think of everything, don't you?" Taylor snarled, handing it back. "Is that a fake, too?"

"Oh, no," he was told, "I borrowed that from Monty, who's been a great help to me in this little scheme as an amateur partner."

He put the bills in his pocket and took out the cigar Taylor had given him.

"Here's your cigar," he said.

Taylor snatched it from him, and biting off the end, stuck it in his mouth. He assumed a brazen air of bravado. "Well," he cried bragging, "it took the biggest man in the secret service to land me, Mr. R. J., but I've got some mighty good pals, in some mighty good places, and they'll come across for me, and don't you forget it. After all, you're not the jury, and all the smart lawyers aren't dead yet."

"I don't think they'll help you this time," Denby said. "I believe you'll still enjoy that winter climate."

"Aw, come on, you dirty grafter," Gibbs cried contemptuously, and with his partner led the broken man away.

Ethel came to his side when they were alone. "Did you really mean it about arranging with Mr. Harrington?" she cried.

He looked down at her tenderly. "Yes," he said. "We've saved her."

"And you are really R. J.?" she exclaimed wonderingly.

"I really am," he returned. "Can't you guess how much I wanted to tell you before? But I couldn't you know, at first, because I thought you might be Taylor's accomplice. And later, I still dared not, because I was under orders with my duty toward my Government. Can you forgive me for making you suffer like that?"

"Forgive you?" she whispered tenderly. "Haven't I said I love you?"

He took her in his arms and kissed her.

"And everything's all right now, isn't it?" she sighed happily.

He looked at her whimsically.

"Except that I'm hungry—are you hungry?"

"Starved," she cried.

"Let's ask for some food," he suggested. "Nothing would gratify Lambart so much. But I don't think I've been so hungry since I was in Paris."

"I wish it were Paris," she said. "Dear Paris, where I first found R. J."

"It shall be, whenever you say," he answered, "and I'll tell you all about R. J. and the lonely life he led till he saw you."

"And to think I could believe for a moment you were a criminal!" she said, self-reproach in her voice, "and even try to trap you!"

"But you've caught me," he said proudly.

"Have I really got you, Steve?" she asked, softly, holding out her arms to him.

THE END

Milton Keynes UK
Ingram Content Group UK Ltd.
UKHW030624061024
449204UK00004B/339